CW00847404

For Europe!

For Europe!

copyright photo on backcover: © Koen Broos
copyright cover design: Peter-Andreas Hassiepen, München
© Carl Hanser Verlag München 2012

ISBN-13: 978-1479261888

Daniel Cohn-Bendit
and Guy Verhofstadt

FOR EUROPE!

Manifesto for a postnational revolution in Europe

followed by an interview by Jean Quatremer

Content

1

Attack is the best means of defence. Europe is wobbling on its legs. Europe is trembling on its foundations. The euro crisis is in full swing. But this crisis is merely a symptom of a much deeper crisis, a crisis with which Europe has long been wrestling. An existential crisis. A multi-faceted crisis.
A "polycrisis", as Edgar Morrin calls it. A crisis which is economic, demographic, ecological, political and institutional all at the same time.

We are being overtaken by the emerging economies at lightning speed, while we ourselves are barely able to create enough growth and innovation. At the same time, Europe is visibly ageing, while the population of the rest of the world is growing at a spectacular pace and is rapidly getting younger. Huge financial resources are needed to wean our economy off the fossil fuels to which it is addicted, but we are unable or, at best, barely able to mobilise them. And when push comes to shove, the European Union is a politically divided continent split up into twenty-seven bits and pieces, and yet we are still required to compete against economic and political powerhouses of the calibre of China, India, Brazil, Russia or the United States. In short, Europe

9

increasingly gives the impression of being a decrepit old lady. A marginalised continent which has difficulty in coping in a new era and a new world. A continent blinkered by too much nationalism. A continent without ambition, without aura and without hope.

The drama is that the European Union is being blamed for all of this. It is the European Union that got us into the euro crisis. It is the European Union that triggered the recession through austerity. It is the European Union that is responsible for the excesses of globalisation. And it is also the European Union that has finally alienated the people from politics. All of this is absurd! Nonsense! It is the Member States who bear full responsibility for today's debacle. It is their failings that have led to the euro crisis. It is also their inconsistency that has triggered the recession. It is their blindness which is causing Europe to decline in the world order, in which we no longer play a role of any significance.

Whatever the case, never before has the European project been under so much pressure. Never before has it openly been questioned whether continuing with European integration makes sense. Never before have the people been so massively opposed to the unification of the European continent. Never before have there been so few political leaders who fully support the European project, who resolutely have a European vision, who are firmly committed to a European future for their country and their people. Pushed into a corner by the euro crisis and Europe's oldest opponent – the Europe of nation states - they at best advocate maintaining the status quo, only keeping what already exists. But the only thing that today's polycrisis shows is that the status quo does not offer a way out. We have a choice. Either we can start to take things seriously by moving towards a genuinely united and federal Europe – not a centralised super-state – or we can cling firmly to the nation state and irrevocably lose any prospect of playing a meaningful role in the globalised world of the 21st century.

Only a frontal attack can now save us. A direct attack on the real cause of this crisis: the unwillingness of the nation states to bring about a genuinely united and federal Europe. In other words, their unwillingness to surrender any more power to a united and federal Europe. The reality in Europe is clear: it is the egotism of the Member States that is now determining Europe's course and not the common European interest, not the interest of all of Europe's citizens and peoples. As long as national interest and egotism prevail, it will be impossible to save Europe.

In order to give Europe a new momentum, we must resolutely play the European card. The card of a continent that has never offered us so much prosperity, so much peace, so many rights and so many prospects. We must not allow purely national considerations to thwart those prospects. We must be aware that, as stated above, attack is the best means of defence. An attack to create more and not less Europe. A choice in favour of a united Europe

11

and not the fragmented and outdated Europe offered by the nation state.

In so doing, we must reject any reforms that are too slow. The situation is too serious for that. We must demand a quantum leap in the direction of a genuinely united and federal Europe. Tiny steps forwards are like the pattering of mice because they will convince neither the people not the markets. Only a different kind of Europe can be persuasive: a federal Europe. Not the Europe of today, the Europe of the nation state, which has been a millstone around the neck of the euro crisis for almost three years. Without fundamentally changing what needs to be changed. Without offering European citizens and peoples renewed hope and new prospects.

We must be aware of how serious the threat is. The threat primarily affects all the people and businesses that are living and/or operating in one of the seventeen countries in the eurozone. Countries who largely owe their current prosperity to the existence of the single European currency. A currency that has ensured that monetary obstacles have been eliminated, that losses on exchange-rate differences are a thing of the past, and that trade in Europe has seen unprecedented growth. That and much more risks being lost if the euro disappears. This would be a true disaster.

How in Heaven's name has it come to this? What went wrong? Why did things turn sour? Let's not beat about the bush. The inventors of the euro and the founders of the eurozone committed a fatal error from the word go. They signed up to the benefits associated with the single currency but were unable to agree on the obligations and how the burdens should be shared out. The benefits were and still are the European single currency itself, the euro, low inflation and low interest rates. The burdens, on the other hand, involve pursuing a strictly integrated economic and fiscal policy, one which is the same in all euro countries. It is all very well to have a single currency, but without establishing a single integrated Europe it is a contradiction and an impossibility.

This is the essence of today's crisis: a shared currency is incompatible with the continued existence of the old nation states, at least in their present form. Consequently, either a European federal state must be created and a post-national Europe come to light, or the European currency must disappear. There is no intermediate solution. But we must also realise that if the eurozone collapses, the European Union itself will be doomed. The eurozone accounts for three-quarters of European GDP. If the euro perishes, so does the Union. In short, it is the very future of Europe that is at stake.

Cherish what unites us, not what divides us. We must be aware that in the world of tomorrow only a united Europe will be able to play a meaningful role. After all, it is clear what the future holds in store. The world is unmistakably on course towards unprecedented unification. A world with as many as five thousand living languages and cultures is now made up of fewer than two hundred states.

And these two hundred states in fact make up ten or so economic powers or alliances. It is they that determine the fate of the world economy.

It was the European states that gave the first impulses towards globalisation. By gradually taking possession of three-quarters of the world through force. By deluding the rest of the world with false hopes of democracy and the rule of law. By developing into the main commercial superpower in the world. But precisely at the moment that other countries in the world are developing into economic empires or joining forces to become genuine conglomerates, the Europeans are retreating into the outdated concept of the nation state. This is a huge strategic mistake. They might as well commit suicide! Because thinking that the nation state is best placed in today's world to guard the economic and financial interests of its citizens and businesses is pure folly. Within twenty years or so, no single European country will still count when it comes to what happens in the world. The club of the richest countries, the so-called G8, will be made up of the United States, China, India, Japan, Brazil, Russia, Mexico and Indonesia. Not a single European country, not even Germany, will belong to it. However, a unified and united Europe is today the most powerful and prosperous continent in the world, and will probably remain so in future. More prosperous than America. More powerful than all the new empires put together.

But there is a second reason why it would be a fundamental error not to speed up European integration: the lightning speed at which economic and financial globalisation is itself progressing. Since the financial crisis of 2008 we have known that globalisation urgently requires a political counterweight in order to function properly. National supervisory bodies are no match against the excesses of multinational financial institutions. They operate at the speed of light on financial markets spanning the entire world. Only a united Europe can play a meaningful role in drawing up a global economic and financial regulatory framework.

Only if Europe is united economically and politically can we have any chance of putting our values and principles on the table and being accepted as equals. Otherwise, it is the interests of India, China and other Asian newcomers which will prevail. So far it has been the North Atlantic world which has steered the rest, sometimes for better, sometimes for worse. This will fundamentally change, especially if Europe is not able to speak with one voice. Then not only will the North Atlantic alliance disappear, the whole European continent will also crumble. Gradually we are becoming an insignificant power factor in a world which is increasingly concentrated around the Pacific. In short, a radical shake-up is essential. Otherwise, our two thousand years of history risks being wiped out.

We must refocus. Those who present the national interest as being diametrically opposed to the interests of Europe and its citizens are making a mistake. Globalisation is irreversible. And within a globalised world the interests of European citizens can only be guaranteed by a strong European Union. It is true that globalisation opens up a wealth of opportunities, just as it is true that it can quickly turn into a tragedy for millions of people. But it is not globalisation *per se* that is the problem. What is is our inability to keep it on course and take control of it.

It must be reiterated that there is no reason to be afraid of globalisation. Rather than seeking to oppose it, we must influence, guide and develop it and give it an ecological and political face. In short, we must create a social, ecological and political globalisation alongside the economic, commercial and financial globalisation we all know. It is an intolerable paradox that political decision-making in this world still lies at the level of nation states, while neither the economic nor the financial world respects state borders. This paradox can only be eliminated by making political decision-making more international, that is by setting up an alternative form of globalisation.

Such a transition towards a global government at world level is not for now. We should not immediately think about installing a world government, although that should remain our ultimate goal. But it is perfectly conceivable for us to draw up and take the necessary political decisions at world level within a global network of large countries and continental alliances. Whether with the G8, the G20, the UN Security Council or the International Monetary

Fund, the large countries should join forces with the main regional organisations so as to take the lead in drafting the political framework within which globalisation should develop.

It is up to the European Union to be a frontrunner in this process. This is not difficult. On the contrary. It is very easy to merge the seats which various EU Member States currently occupy in those organisations into one seat intended for representatives of the entire European Union, in the UN Security Council, the World Bank, the IMF and all other international organisations. The fact that, sixty years after the creation of the European Union, there should be countries – such as France and Great Britain – who do not wish to consider this is rather pathetic. Both continue to cling desperately to their outdated prerogatives without really realising that they no longer play a significant role. It is a "spasm" of extreme short-sightedness because in this way they are denying the European Union a unique opportunity to fully benefit from its size and to actually have some clout in determining world events.

We must look ahead, not behind. Just think what the world will look like in twenty or thirty years. And not what the world looked like twenty or thirty years ago. The world's population has trebled since 1927. There were two billion then, and seven billion now. In forty years, it will certainly have risen to ten billion. But it is just as revolutionary that half of the world's population now lives in urban conurbations.

17

And this proportion is likely to rise to almost three-quarters by the end of this century.

We are witnessing an unprecedented dual demographic revolution. The world has never had so many people and so many urban residents. With all the consequences this has for the intolerable juxtaposition of rich and poor. For employment and food supply. For education and health. For our energy needs and our mobility. For everybody's safety. For everything that we produce and consume. For the environment and the impending climate change. Most of the problems which people have to deal with today and in the near future are global. What people and nations do or do not do will have an ever greater impact on the entire planet. Individual states will barely have any clout in tackling these global challenges. Unless they are as big as China, India, the United States or Russia. Powers, indeed "empires", that are in fact made up of many nations. In short, in tomorrow's world it will not be individual European countries but only Europe or the European Union that will still play a meaningful role. That is, of course, if we manage to pull in the same direction. If we are able to speak with one voice.

But there is more at stake. More Europe is not only necessary in order to tackle the planet's problems with a chance of success, but also in order at all cost to secure our position in the world and to safeguard our ways of life, however much they may vary. More Europe is the only guarantee of maintaining our own prosperity, social achievements and cultural diversity. Indeed, in politics it is the case that we risk losing our acquired rights precisely as a result of our inability to find appropriate answers to today's challenges. In politics, inertia always leads to aggression. In short, to the loss of what is most valuable to us.

Many are convinced the opposite is true. On both the right and the left it is fashionable to extol the virtues of sovereign nation states. The people who do so cling on to the old sovereign countries as the best guarantee against social uncertainty and insecurity. People are becoming unemployed, losing their benefits, being made redundant and living on the edge of a society that had paid the price of world globalisation. In contrast, the nation state that is glorified is a haven of peace and prosperity. A place which, alongside an upbringing and an education, also guarantees an income and social protection. On the other hand, the European Union is pilloried, branded a sort of fifth column which wants to subject people to an economic order which completely removes the social context from under their feet.

But they have chosen the wrong enemy. However understandable their criticism is of the way the world is developing and of society, the solutions they provide are far from the right ones. Just as the old nation states have not seemed able to combat the export of jobs, they are completely unable to protect the social gains achieved in the globalised world of tomorrow. We are seeing this every day. In Greece.

In Portugal. In Spain. Only the European Union is able to develop strategies to combat social dumping, to guarantee the social rights of all European citizens and to eradicate poverty. In the same way that it is only Europe that can force the BRICS countries (Brazil, Russia, India, China and South Africa) and other emerging countries on the planet to create the environmental and social protection that is vital and without which the earth will become uninhabitable.

In any case, it is absurd to claim that we are able to keep world events outside our national borders. That we can build a wall around each of our countries. A wall of this nature does not exist and can never be erected. Only a strong and united Europe operating on an equal footing with world competition is able to guarantee the prosperity of its citizens and the continent's democratic, social and cultural achievements. In short, only a post-national Europe is able to ensure that our ideals of "liberty, equality and fraternity" remain firmly anchored.

2

We should not resign ourselves to the current state of affairs. The euro crisis does not in any way indicate that the introduction of the single European currency was a mistake. Or that the European Union is doomed to failure. Do not let yourself be misled. This is not a crisis about the euro or the single European currency *per se*. What is true is that, at the outset, there was a serious flaw, an almost fatal design fault in the way the single currency was constructed. When the euro was officially launched on 1 January 2002, those who had initiated it were well aware that it would not work without an integrated European economic and fiscal policy. But because they could not agree on how this union should be organised, they persuaded themselves that an integrated economic and fiscal policy would naturally emerge as a result of the euro. This was a grave miscalculation. Ten years later, it appears that, unfortunately, virtually nothing has been done to establish a political, economic and fiscal union. The euro crisis was thus foreseeable. It was plain to see in all the handbooks dedicated to the European Union. Perhaps states can exist without a currency, but a currency cannot exist without a state.

Without a public authority which is strong and credible enough to enforce discipline and solidarity, a currency is doomed to disappear.

Three years after the outbreak of the euro crisis, a crisis which is still raging at full intensity, the Member States still believe that they can do without it. We still have 17 governments in the eurozone, 17 finance ministers, 17 central banks, 17 different bond markets. We still do not have a European Government. The Member States still think that they can keep the single currency together without surrendering massive new powers, i.e. a new dose of "national sovereignty", to the European institutions. They still think they have managed to escape having to set up a genuine federal Union. They are mistaken. Only if we establish a federal Union, based on a European Government which determines economic, budgetary and fiscal policy and is able to impose rules on all eurozone Member States is the single European currency feasible. Just as it is also obvious that the European Union itself will only survive if such a Government is anchored in a genuine European democracy brought about through enhanced parliamentary institutions and control involving the citizens. It is not about replacing one technocracy with another.

We should unmask the true face of the euro crisis. It is not a Greek crisis. It is certainly not a crisis of Portugal, Ireland, Italy, Spain or one of the other countries which currently finds itself in the firing line. It is true that Greece has accumulated an enormous debt mountain which it is scarcely able to repay. That Athens committed fraud on a large scale. It is also true that Greek society lives off a grey economy and is poisoned by political clientelism. But this does not even start to explain why the euro got into such deep water.

The United States has a public debt which is somewhat higher than that of the euro countries, but that does not seem to make any difference to the value of the dollar. Japan even has the highest public debt in the world, but nobody doubts the strength of the yen. What is more, the Japanese today pay the lowest interest rates in the world despite having the highest public debt. How can that be explained? The answer is that behind the yen and the dollar stands one solid authority, one government and one administration. Nobody doubts the ability of Japan or the United States to generate the necessary incomes and pay their interest.

Things are radically different with the euro and the European Union. European political leaders and the heads of state and government of various countries, with France and Germany at the top, have clearly had doubts in recent years about their readiness to bail out struggling euro countries. The consequence has been that confidence in those countries has plummeted. Which in turn has led to falling ratings and rising interest rates. In the meantime, it is no longer inconceivable that there are countries that will actually go under. Especially as the European Union barely has any budgetary leeway or own resources to bail them out.

But it is not just solidarity that the eurozone is lacking. There is also a lack of discipline – the other prerequisite for maintaining a monetary area. Everybody has long known that the Greeks have been unable to pay their bills. But nobody worried about it. And least of all France and Germany, who just a few years ago themselves trampled on the budgetary rules without being punished for doing so. Without either of them having to pay even the tiniest fine. Either France and Germany had good reasons and the Stability Pact should have been changed, or sanctions should have been taken immediately. In any case, by not doing so, it became crystal clear to everybody that the eurozone's so-called strict budgetary rules were a joke. Not something to be reckoned with. And certainly not anything to make a fuss about. Ultimately the eurozone seems to be built largely on quicksand, with rising interest rates – the so-called spreads – and further increasing indebtedness as a direct result. One thing is now clear: without solidarity and discipline, a currency is unsustainable. And the experience of the last few years has taught us that the Member States, in other words the potential sinners, are unable to force those virtues onto the other sinners. Only independent European institutions - the European Commission and the European Central Bank – are able to do that, provided of course that they come under the direct supervision of a democratic parliament.

More than in any other monetary zone, discipline is vital to the eurozone. And this for the very simple reason that, unlike the United States,

Europe hardly has a credible federal budget, i.e. its own financial resources to be able to guarantee the cohesion of the monetary zone. If California goes bankrupt, or another American state accumulates excessive debt, this does not in any way spell the end of the single American currency, the dollar. Not so in Europe – the euro falters the minute a small economy like that of Greece, which accounts for barely two per cent of European wealth, topples.

Let us certainly not argue that what is obviously wrong is right. You have to be blind not to see that the European Union is barely coping with the most menacing crisis since its creation. Almost three years after the euro crisis broke out in Athens in December 2009 we have got nowhere. All attempts to stem it end in failure. 'It is only thanks to the European Central Bank that we are keeping our heads above water. It is buying up massive quantities of government bonds of the countries in need and has already pumped hundreds of billions of euros into our under-capitalised banks, which treat each other with distrust.

Not that our heads of state and government are not taking decisions. On the contrary. After months of hesitation, they have set up an emergency fund, although they did have their backs against the wall. Enhanced European monitoring of the Member States' budgets has been introduced, together with enhanced supervision of banks and of financial and banking products. For the first time, automatic sanctions are provided for against

Member States who allow their finances to derail. This is by no means an unnecessary luxury because there are barely three Member States – Finland, Estonia and Luxembourg - that actually comply with the strict rules of the eurozone. Rules that require that no Member State may accumulate debt greater than 60% of its GDP or tolerate a budget deficit of more than 3%. Finally, the Member States will soon be required to enshrine the "golden rule", a requirement which will force them to keep their budgets in balance, into their constitutions. Only these decisions have hitherto made no or too little impression on the outside world. And certainly not on the financial markets. Because they came too late. And above all because they did not go far enough. They have been judged "too little, too late".

Rules apply to everybody or to nobody. What is particularly dragging the euro down is the disbelief on the part of the financial markets that the (amended) rules will now suddenly be applied. A rule is only credible if it is strictly and consistently complied. And nobody has forgotten that Europe's largest countries, Germany and France, have themselves squarely flouted them. Apparently the European rules were not rules in the literal sense but a sort of voluntary recommendation or guidelines that each Member State did what it wanted with. The consequence was that virtually no action was taken against the perpetrators. Why should smaller countries such as Greece and Portugal be punished if the two largest countries allowed their budget deficits to rise above the required three per cent without punishment? Not that the budget deficits immediately had serious consequences. Growth was strong, and inflation and interest rates were low. The financial crisis of 2008 was far off. That all changed when Lehman Brother became the first large bank to go belly up. A financial tsunami crossed the Atlantic and forced European countries to inject huge amounts of public money into their insurance companies and banks.

Since 2008, the EU Member States have pumped no less than € 4,600 billion into their financial institutions in the form of direct grants and public guarantees. And that is not to mention the hundreds of billions of euros that have been spent on the various recovery and relaunch plans. It is no wonder that, a year later, the financial crisis which originated in the United States would lead to a genuine debt crisis in Europe. It suddenly looked like not all European economies would withstand the tsunami. Some euro countries were strong. Above all Germany. Others were weak. They had not adjusted or reformed since they had succumbed to the drug of low interest rates. And then there was the safety net of the common currency, the euro. But what was lacking was a common economic, budgetary and fiscal framework which at the same time obliged the euro countries to implement fundamental adjustments and reforms. Since the launch of the euro, the difference in economic performance between the countries had only grown. European leaders had increasingly widened the gap between the north and south of Europe. We did have a monetary union but still no economic or fiscal union, let alone a political union. And the events of the last three years have shown just how crucial they are.

What we need in order to turn the tide. Organising meetings of heads of state and government as regularly as clockwork seems in each case to have been a waste of time. The Franco-German Summits, those get-togethers between the French President and German Chancellor about which so much fuss is made, have also not brought any solace for some time. At most they manage to calm the markets for 24 or 48 hours. After which it all starts up again. And the fever runs higher than ever before. What we need in order to turn the tide is a completely different order. The time for papering over the cracks is finally over. Simply plugging the holes will not be enough to save the euro. Nobody now believes in the inter-Governmental model, whereby Member States supposedly monitor and sanction each other. This method has not worked in the past. Why should it work in the future?

What we need is a genuine revolution. The establishment of genuine federal Union with supranational European institutions. Community institutions which have the power to determine economic, budgetary and fiscal policy for the entire eurozone. Institutions which are given the means to truly enforce compliance with the rules. Without the Member States being able to throw

28

a spanner in the works. In concrete terms, this means transforming the European Commission as quickly as possible into a genuine European Government. With European ministers who we today call commissioners. Monitored by a European Parliament with enhanced powers. Including the right to initiate legislation itself. Only in this way can we get the Union out of the mess it finds itself in. Once again, the European Council of Heads of State and Government is unable to do this. Whether they like to hear it or not.

The European Council is nothing other than a syndicate of national interests. Those sitting on it are merely there to defend the egotistical self-interests of their country. And certainly not to secure the European interest. The interest of the citizens and peoples of Europe. The European Council can never be the guarantee for, let alone the driving force behind, more Europe or the establishment of a federal Europe. The European citizens must do that themselves. By clearly opting for a pro-European political project. By bringing a majority to power that resolutely votes in favour of a post-national and federal future for the old continent. Let us not delude ourselves. This is only the first step towards a fundamentally different approach. The way out of the euro crisis demands more fundamental reforms. Such as the reform of the existing emergency fund into a genuine European Monetary Fund based on the model of the International Monetary Fund. This would rule out matters being blocked by one Member State. Also needed is the establishment of a

29

European public treasury that can issue euro-bonds. Only then will it be possible to truly turn the debt crisis around. Because only then will we be able to assure the markets that discipline and solidarity are not just empty words but the unshakable pillars of our unified monetary system. And only then will the euro be able to develop into the most important reserve currency in the world.

We should not just be focussed on austerity but also investing in new growth. One thing has now become clear: we will not overcome the crisis through austerity alone. Europe needs growth. Sound public finances are of course vital to guarantee growth in the medium term. But they will not make the crisis disappear overnight. On the contrary. There is a real danger that what is happening in Greece or other countries will bring the entire Union into a downward spiral. Massive cuts are affecting economic prospects. Incomes are rapidly falling. This will force us to make even more cuts, which in turn leads to lower growth. In short, initiatives are needed alongside austerity to generate growth and prosperity. And given the poor state of public finances in most countries, meaning that there are no funds to take such initiatives, only Europe can provide the solution.

This requires two radical interventions: a credible European budget and the establishments of a large euro-bond market. The latter is necessary in order to attract as many savers and investors from inside and outside Europe as possible. Europeans are big savers. In many Member States they are sitting on wealth which exceeds the country's GDP. But trust is lacking. Savers fear that the money that they hand over to most Member States will never be repaid. It would be one of the aims of a European bond market to restore that trust, not only in order to cover the euro countries debts at a lower cost but also in order to assemble the funds necessary to relaunch the economy. Necessary to put Europe back on the path of growth. Which is itself necessary to eventually get rid of our debt mountain.

The driving force behind new growth in Europe must be the complete transformation of our economic apparatus, which today is completely addicted to fossil fuels. This would enable us to kill three birds with one stone. A non-fossil-based economy could make an enormous contribution to effectively reducing greenhouse gases. This radical change would also stimulate sustainable economic growth and thus put Europe back on the world economic map.

Invest in the radical change of our production and growth model. It is the economy which requires us to fundamentally review the development model which has hitherto prevailed in the industrialised world. The ecological ravages caused by our current means of trading are having dramatic consequences. They will considerably worsen the current economic and social crisis if we do not quickly step into action. Climate change, the loss of biodiversity, the depletion of the main raw materials and shortages

31

of water, food and energy are the ingredients for an unprecedented ecological crisis. A crisis which is inextricably linked to the current economic malaise in Europe and the global population explosion. For decades we have been living at our planet's expense. For generations we have produced and consumed too much, thinking that raw materials were inexhaustible. Our biosphere has been ruined. And inequalities in the world have increased rather than decreased. 80% of raw materials in the world are consumed by barely 20% of the population. And what is most unfair is the fact that it is precisely the poorest countries who are least to blame for the ecological damage who are now paying the heaviest price.

A complete shift towards a green and sustainable economy is essential. This is the only way of sustainably boosting our competitiveness and thus reviving the European economy. Millions of new jobs can already be created in the renewable energy and energy efficiency sectors alone, especially if Europe reduces its greenhouse gas emissions by 30% rather than the planned 20%. Reducing our consumption through more energy efficiency must thus be the cornerstone of future policy. In this context, a major housing renovation project should be established immediately at European level, the benefits of which must be felt straightaway in the form of new jobs which will not be transferred abroad and a perceptible reduction in family budgets resulting from lower energy bills. In other words, combating climate change and creating employment are not mutually exclusive. On the contrary, economics and ecology go hand in hand.

At a time when Europe is confronted with rapidly rising unemployment, the "green economy" offers an excellent opportunity to turn the tide. Europe definitely needs a "green deal", an all-embracing ecological modernisation of our society covering a whole range of different sectors: industry, construction, the renovation of public and private buildings, private and public transport, renewable energy, agriculture, the protection of biodiversity and waste treatment. All sectors which will be able to benefit immediately from the creation of new jobs which will remain in Europe, new innovation and a renewed independence from raw materials. A "green deal" is the only way out of the crisis if we at least wish not to slide deeper into a recession that will have dramatic consequences for our prosperity and economic position in the world.

3

Let us not be discouraged. The European Union was probably the best thing that happened to the old continent in the last millennium. After the horrors of the Second World War, the European continent was in ruins. It is by striving towards European unification that Europe has been able to rise from the ashes in less than sixty years. Without European integration, this would probably have been impossible. With a divided European market, it would in any case have taken much longer to achieve the standard of living which we now have. The European Union is a major project which is directly opposed to nationalism and conservatism and is consistent with everything that Europe has created in recent centuries: the Enlightenment, the rule of law, human rights, the free economy, political democracy and social security. Each one of them major developments which sprouted in Europe and went on to conquer the whole world. This is again the case now with the idea of European unification.

Unification would prove that tenacious nationalistic reflexes and centuries-old rivalries can be overcome.

First people organised themselves on the basis of local communities, and then in regional associations. Over the last two centuries, we have developed so-called national entities. European Unification shows that this is not the end of history. The future undoubtedly lies in international cooperation. Even more, in the creation of supranational social institutions covering an entire continent. The European Union is a shining example of this. The torch that has also encouraged and inspired other continents to go down the path of regional cooperation. Mercosur in Latin America, Asean in South-East Asia, and the African Union in Africa. It would be an enormous setback if the European project were to fail. Not only for ourselves, but also and above all for developments on this planet. Because it would be a fatal blow to multilateralism.

At this particular moment, it would be a catastrophe. Combating climate change, ensuring sustainable development and fighting poverty are all international matters that are almost at a standstill. The failure of the European project would make things even worse. Even more, in the four corners of the world we would again have to reckon with rivalries and increased tensions between different countries. Even large-scale trade conflicts or new international wars could not be ruled out. Conflicts that would increasingly be about water and energy. Conflicts concerning the gas reserves in the Mediterranean, for example, such as between Cyprus and Turkey. Or the rich energy supplies under the North Pole which might be extractable as a result of climate change, which are already leading to serious tensions between Denmark, Norway, Russia, Canada and the United States.

European unification was always a source of hope and inspiration. This is not the time to succumb to euro-scepticism and abandon ship or let it capsize. This is not the time to falter. There is a lot to be done, in Europe and the world. We Europeans were the first to proclaim universal rights and freedoms and to elevate democracy as the standard. Today we must defend and spread these values. And we can only succeed if we further integrate our continent. Only in this way can we contribute to the further "internationalisation" of law by consolidating existing and developing new instruments. The International Criminal Court and the principle of "the responsibility to protect" have ushered in a new period in which sovereignty extends far beyond the national state. The beginning, one might say, of a universally applicable, cosmopolitan legal order.

We must recognise that peace in Europe has never been permanently achieved. There was a time when wars prevailed in Europe: between one city and another, between counties and dutchies, between vassals and lieges, between one country and another. No other continent has provided so many battlefields or seen so many armed conflicts in the last thousand years than Europe. The Second World War was the last to be fought in Europe. Since 1945 Europe has seen no more wars, apart from the Balkan War, and even that conflict – itself an anachronism, a relic of the

Second World War and the division decided on at Yalta - now finally belongs to the past since Croatia and Slovenia have joined the European Union. The precursor for the entry of all Balkan countries into the European order.

Moreover, no continent is better equipped to renounce its violent past and strive for a more peaceful world than ours. It was the enemies of freedom – communism, fascism and Nazism – that plunged Europe into the greatest misery in the twentieth century. Let us not allow these ghosts to take the upper hand again. The heirs of communism, fascism and Nazism are not dead but are today merely hiding in the shadow of many populist and xenophobic movements. Let us not forget the greatest lesson from our history: what has happened in the past can always happen again. Don't think that history does not repeat itself. We are no better or smarter or cleverer than our ancestors. Just as we are no worse, more stupid or more clumsy. We simply have to be cautious. We must not allow our rights and freedoms to be restricted. React in time. Don't wait until it is too late.

Let's take Hungary as an example. What is happening there is an outright disgrace. And an even greater disgrace is the fact that the reaction of the European Union is so weak, almost non-existent. The freedom of religion, the freedom of the press and the freedom of information are fundamental values which should not be tampered with. No single concept, not even that of the "holy Hungarian nation", can be invoked in order to confine or restrict them. Rights and freedoms are absolute values, values which cannot be haggled over or negotiated. They are also rare commodities which have cost many human lives to obtain. It would be a disaster if we should lose them because we are not paying attention or, even worse, because we are too lenient with those who would undermine them.

Defuse the false rhetoric of Europe's enemies. Europe's opponents of the past are still its enemies today: the nationalists, the conservatives and the populists. The nationalists want each nation to live in its own state. As though they are best divided up into separate compartments. For Europe, which currently has forty-four countries, this would require a further division into more than three hundred and fifty autonomous Member States, mini-states like Andorra, Liechtenstein or San Marino. Africa, which currently has around fifty states, would end up with more than two thousand small national entities. It would be a nightmare! It would in any case lead to violence of unprecedented proportions. Because people do not live or remain living within their own so-called national borders. This is a myth. They do not live in neatly separate compartments. People have always lived in ethnically mixed regions. Often they will marry somebody from a different area. Out of choice or in order to make a livelihood, they move to places where they can find work or which offer them better prospects for the future.

The world currently has 193 national states. If we were to go down the nationalist line, there would, according to ethnologists, be at least five thousand. But these five thousand "states" would bring little solace now that more than half of mankind lives in large cities, i.e. in a mixed environmental in which languages, religions and peoples in any case live side by side. The modern multicultural society is living proof that the nationalist delusion is entirely obsolete.

We should not waste any more time on patching up a distant past. Not that this past is not important. Of course it is! We can learn a lot from it. But that is not what nationalism does. Nationalism does not learn from history. It denies history by constantly rewriting and manipulating it. What nationalism does again and again is to feed upon history. Justifying itself to the level of absurdity by harking back to mythical heroes and memorable if not decisive battles. Memories that serve purely to satisfy their fantasies. Memories from a distant dark past, preferably from the Dark Ages, so that they can project their prejudices of today without too much contradiction.

Like Joan of Arc, the subject of devotion of all French nationalists, who at the age of 17 is said to have saved France from the English during the Hundred Years War, but about whose true identity opinion still differs among historians. Spanish nationalists venerate El Cid, the Christian "liberator" of Valencia in 1094. The spiritual father of the "Reconquista", which ended with the Arabs being driven out of Granada and the expulsion from the country of 800,000 Jews, treated as though they were dogs. The Scottish nationalists revere like no other their victory over the English at Bannockburn in 1314 under the leadership of Robert the Bruce. And Flemish nationalists still celebrate the victory on 11 July 1302 of ordinary Flemish pikemen over the "fine fleur" of the French Army at Kortrijk.

The nationalists even celebrate defeats. In Hungary a historical defeat to the Turks at Mohacs in 1526, which heralded a 150-year Turkish tutelage over the Hungarian Plain, is still revered. In Serbia, there is no more important a day than 28 June 1389, the date of their historic defeat to the Kosovar Merelveld. It was also the first day of 500 years of Turkish-Ottoman rule over the Balkans.

But what message do all these memorable dates give us? Will even one of our problems today be solved by harking back to the clash of arms between our forefathers? Will the world function better tomorrow? No, solutions to our problems should not be sought in the deeds of our venerable ancestors. Solutions must be found in the world of today. A world that throws up something new every day. A world that each day creates new problems but also provides new solutions.

Let us celebrate the men and women who have created Europe. Those who insist on worshipping heroes or idolising symbols would do better to revere our real heroes, the European heroes. The heroes of today. The heroes who have created the European Union. The heroes who have put a stop to the delusion of the nationalists: Monnet, Schuman, Adenauer, Spaak. De Gasperi and Spinelli, the fathers of

European democracy. Let us honour them rather than continuing to idolise our national past.

Why not let them adorn our euro banknotes? Rather than the dull, worn-out notes of today featuring shadowy buildings which in fact relate to nothing. With arches and bridges which do not even resemble any of the beautiful monuments of which Europe has so many. Let us instead see the likeness of those who not so long ago gave form and content to the vision of Europe. And while we are at it, let us also get rid of the accursed treaties in which even the European flag and the European anthem were no longer given a place. Our fatherland is now Europe. Our national anthem is "Ode to Joy". And our flag is that of the twelve yellow stars on an azure background.

Let us remember that conservatives and populists are only pursuing their fantasies. For conservatives, it is like a law of nature. To be happy, people must be chained to their own habitat, their own environment. Everything outside that small circle alienates people, makes them anxious, restless and ultimately unhappy. Populists go a step further. In order to ward off the threat from outside, resist the baleful influence of foreign languages, religions and peoples, everything that is different must be suppressed or undone. Populism interprets the "gut feeling" of a "threatened" nation. But is the nation actually "threatened"? Is the presence of other languages, peoples and religions not in fact something that enriches the nation? Is the "homogeneous" nation not merely a delusion which is disconnected from reality. And what about following one's "gut feeling"? Is that a desirable starting point in politics? Would it not be better to follow our reason and our experience, which both teach us that the idea of race is merely a groundless abstraction? That there are in fact only human beings, people who have the same basic rights irrespective of which language they speak, which religion they profess or which nationality they belong to.

Following one's so-called gut feeling in public affairs will sooner or later merely lead to discrimination, war and persecution. And the one thing we have had enough of in Europe is war and persecution, broken families, massacred minorities, countries reduced to rubble and flattened cities. In the twentieth century alone, war in Europe caused the deaths of at least fifty million people. There is not a single family in Europe that has not lost a member to war. Entire peoples, above all the Jews, have been decimated. Who wants that to happen again? The populists would of course deny that they do. But we see them at work whenever they come to power. Sooner or later nationalism leads to modern versions of the same tragedies. We would have to be naïve to think otherwise.

Break the silence that has surrounded the European project for years. Sweep away the indifference which eventually makes every society waste away. The draining lethargy that brings down all social institutions. We must dare to think European again.

43

We must dare to defend European viewpoints again. Bring the European Project up to date for the Europe and world of tomorrow. We must again be as creative as the pioneers of the European idea were in the past. And above all, we must defend it against all those who oppose it. Attack them head on. Fight against nationalists, conservatives, populists. Confront them with the unimaginable dramatic consequences of a collapse of the European continent. Make them realise what a return to nationalism will mean. Explain to them what the cost of non-Europe is, of a Europe broken down into even smaller units, as represented by the rat catchers of Hamlyn for whom even the existing states are too large. Work out what the demise of the euro would cost. It would mean massive contraction of our wealth two to three times greater than the economic downturn which followed the collapse of Lehman.

Ridicule those who only see Europe as a loose collection of old fatherlands. Unmask the conservatives who essentially just want to eliminate democracy. And above all put to shame the populists who think that they know what "the people" are thinking. Politicians who follow their voters in their basest instincts. Instead of leading them towards what elevates us. Democracy means being ahead of public opinion, not blindly following it out of purely opportunistic or electoral considerations. Democracy means relying on intelligence, the reason of the individual, not his basest instincts. Involving and letting him or her decide about the future emancipation of society.

Let us celebrate the fact that practically every society is multicultural. Five thousand years ago, the first people settled in Mesopotamia, creating an urban environment which was already multicultural. The city embraced races and cultures. And this is all the more true today. More than half of the world lives in urban conurbations. A hundred years ago this was at most one in ten. Two hundred years ago barely two per cent. Today only isolated villages in remote areas in distant countries are homogeneous. Moreover, the increasingly multicultural nature of cities and states presents no threat to people or society. People today, just like modern society, have multiple characteristics. A layered identity which they increasingly determine themselves. The multicultural nature of modern society has become a fact, a self-evidence. Not something that can succeed or fail, as Angela Merkel and Nicolas Sarkozy, above all, recently decreed. But something that just happens to exist. Something that should not be undone.

Instead of giving in to our fears or phobias, we should instead open our eyes to the richness that multiculturalism can offer. We should acknowledge the virtues of multiculturalism, its contributions to the development of social intelligence, i.e. the ability to deal with other people. Let us protect multiculturalism, just as we wish to secure the universal values of human rights and democracy on which they are based. In short, let us cherish social ideals rather than focus on what divides and separates us.

45

An open and multicultural society is an inexhaustible source of new insights. It liberates us from our arrogance and vanity. As if our way of living and thinking is automatically the best or indeed the only way. What biological variety is for all life on earth, multicultural diversity is for every form of society. This does not mean that every form of culture should be tolerated. Certainly not when the fundamental principles of human rights and democracy are trampled on as a result of political opportunism or on the basis of ethnic/nationalistic or fundamentalist motives, or even worse, with ulterior criminal motives. Female circumcision, the stoning of adulterous wives, xenophobia, slavery, human trafficking, organ trafficking, homophobia, all other forms of discrimination based on a person's nature, whether or not propagated by fundamentalist movements ... there are so many violations which show that the struggle for human rights and an open multicultural society is far from won.

Let us walk in the footsteps of the pioneers of European thinking. The inventors, writers, voyagers of discovery. The many creative men and women who have inspired mankind over the last five hundred years. Never before did one continent have such influence in the world. But Europe's success also owed much to what was borrowed from other cultures and civilisations, be it the compass, printing or gunpowder – the three elements at the basis of Europe's great leap forwards in the fifteenth century, which were not European but Chinese inventions. But it was Europe which turned them into instruments of global progress.

This European ingenuity and imagination is virtually extinct today. The gangrene of nationalism has - alas - permanently damaged it. Kafka or Einstein are unimaginable in today's Europe. Their descendants died in the gas chambers of Auschwitz and Treblinka. Thanks to the nationalists and populists Europe has in just a single century been transformed from an ethnic and cultural melting pot into a monotonous collection of mono-cultural and mono-ethnic islands. Only Poles now live in Poland. Hungarians in Hungary. Germans in Germany, many returning from the four corners of Lithuania, Romania and Russia to where their ancestors emigrated from centuries ago. There is little left in the belly of Europe of that mishmash of languages, cultures and religions which led to all that imagination and ingenuity. Sacrificed together with all its exciting diversity on the altar of the narrowest nationalist ideology.

The centre of ingenuity and imagination finally moved after the Second World War to the other side of the Atlantic, to the multicultural land of immigration *par excellence*: the United States of America. Can the curse on Europe every be undone? Can the clock be turned back? The answer is yes. If Europe frees itself from the straitjacket of nationalism. If Europe again embraces the multiculturalism it always had. If Europe resolutely reopens itself to outside influences and thereby become a beacon of inventiveness and imagination.

Let us again acknowledge the need for migration. It is only through migration that Europe will in future be able to maintain its prosperity. After all, Europe is visibly ageing. For one thing, there are more older than younger people living in most European Member States. The number of over-sixties in Europe is increasing each year in Europe by two million, while the number of those in employment falls by one million. In the coming decade it is therefore likely that millions of job vacancies will arise, millions of available jobs which cannot be filled. In these circumstances, it will be impossible for Europe to maintain its current standard of living. Instead of accepting the obvious and considering solutions based on the establishment of a European migration strategy, our political decision-makers are moving completely in the opposite direction. By seeking to renationalise Schengen, they are attacking head on the principle of common access to and movement within the European area. This is a position which betrays a distressing lack of solidarity with future generations. Because it will be they who have to deal with the dramatic consequences of the falling birth rate in Europe.

Meanwhile, the inevitable ageing of Europe stands in stark contrast to the rapid rejuvenation of the rest of the world. About a year ago, at the end of October 2011, the seven billionth person was born somewhere in the world. The global population will probably rise to ten billion within a few decades. Two billion of the seven billion world inhabitants are under twenty. In the Arab world, 60% of the population is under thirty. This accelerating growth and rejuvenation of the world's population is best understood if one considers that the six billionth person is today just 12 years old, the fifth billion 24, the fourth billion 36, the third billionth 51 and the second billionth 84. Anybody of our age today was therefore born at a time when there were not even three billion people in the world. We have together seen almost a tripling of the world's population.

It is not so much the number of people on earth that creates hunger, the depletion of the earth's resources or climate change but the way in which we produce and consume and organise our planet. As Mahatma Gandhi was aware almost a hundred years ago, "earth provides enough to satisfy every man's needs, but not every man's greed". But the demographic pressure is no longer sustainable in many countries. Huge numbers of educated people under thirty, particularly in the Arab world, have no job and see on TV and the Internet how things are in other parts of the world. They too want a job, an income and a decent place to live. They too demand the rights and freedoms that are self-evident to us. Europe does not have a choice. Our ageing world needs these young people. And young people elsewhere in the world need the prospect of being able to live a long, active, healthy, peaceful and equitable life.

We must at all events turn our backs on the prophets of doom who seek to return to the time of old national certainties. Nations and peoples do not live neatly alongside each other, safely protected behind so-called borders. What borders would and could exist on a continent on which, over the centuries, countless wars have continually shifted them around? There are no natural borders. Since the first anthropoids swarmed across the world from Africa in a distant past, nobody can call themselves "the first" anywhere. Migration and national relocation have always existed. It is states that draw borders, not peoples. And all the great empires that this world has seen throughout its history were based on a mixture of numerous languages and peoples. With people and communities living all jumbled up.

In short, despite the nationalistic rhetoric, the borders of nations and states never coincide. Which is also the reason why nationalism has plunged Europe into so many wars. Frantic efforts to establish borders between ethnically pure nations and peoples have invariably resulted in a bloodbath. With Auschwitz as the most extreme consequence of what an exaggerated and derailed nationalism can lead to.

We should remember what we have to thank the European Union for. We will again consider what is at stake. The first half of the 20th century was the bloodiest half century in Europe's history. Europe was the backdrop to two world wars. In the same period, Europe conjured up communism, fascism and Nazism. A demonic trio which held the entire continent in its grip and which almost destroyed it. By contrast, the second half of the 20th century has been the most peaceful, most free, most prosperous and most social half century Europe has ever seen. These golden times have a name: the European Union.

An idea so attractive that the European Union would gradually enchant the entire continent. Without a single cannon or gun being fired, it grew from 6 to 9 and then to 10, 12, 15, 25 and 27 Member States. With the accession of the Balkan countries, it will soon rise to more than thirty. And this without a single country being forced to join. What no conqueror was ever able to unite with weapons has emerged over the last half century spontaneously, off its own bat, as if those involved were somehow drawn to each other. Inspired by visionary statesmen, bridge-builders, who first brought about reconciliation between France and Germany. Those "natural enemies" who had fought three wars against each other between 1870 and 1945. There later came reconciliation between north and south: Spain, Portugal, Greece. And later, after the implosion of the Soviet Union, between east and west: Poland, Romania, Bulgaria, Hungary, the Czech Republic, Slovakia and the Baltic States. We must cherish such an extraordinary vision: the unification of the European continent. Particularly in dangerous times when everything looks like overturning. But the job is not done. There is still much to do.

We must force our European "leaders" to have a conscience. Europeans have been missionaries.

Often of evil. The Crusades. The conquest of Latin America, during which the indigenous people were trodden under foot and massacred. Later, European and North America became the stage for French and American missionary zeal. Just as messianic, but this time in a secular sense. True revolutionaries who sought to spread the values of the Enlightenment and the fire of the American and French Revolutions across the world. From France, a new calendar was even introduced. American revolutionaries fanatically proclaimed America's "manifest destiny", their common calling to create a better world at least on the new continent.

This French and American messianism certainly had its bad points. But they also laid the ground for human rights. Universal rights and freedoms which would gradually be adopted and accepted by the entire world. Neither America nor Europe has since lived up to this legacy. Such as during the Arab Spring, when Americans and Europeans were too cowardly to get right behind the uprisings and only reluctantly supported the brave men and women standing up for freedom and democracy. Let us force America and Europe to have a conscience again. What large parts of the world are now demanding, and the peoples in the Middle East in particular, is what we Europeans and Americans showed them, and what we have been proclaiming for more than two centuries, that all people and nations are basically the same and are free. This is our best gift to the world. Even though from time to time we Europeans and Americans cut deep into the flesh. We cannot deny other nations and states what we ourselves take for granted. Human rights and democratic freedoms are universal. They are not Western privileges. They are fundamental achievements to which all people and nations on this planet have an unconditional right and access.

Let us not accept the biggest lie that the nation states continue to tell their citizens, i.e. that they are the foundation of the European Union. That the European Union is in fact a confederation or loose association of states. A sort of United Nations of Europe. Instead of a United States of Europe, i.e. a federal union with a federal authority and federal rules. The nuclei of Europe are not its nations. The nuclei of Europe are its citizens. One of the core aims of European politics should not be the pursuit of the self-interest of the national Member States. The core aim should be to secure the European interest, the interest of the citizens and peoples of Europe. The European Union is a supranational and not an international institution, and has been since the outset. It was the supranational High Authority which determined coal and steel policy in the 1950s, not the six Member States of the ECSC at the time. The same applied to the EEC and Euratom and to the later European Union.

The European Commission and the European Parliament make up the highest European institutions. Alongside the European Council of Heads of State and Government, of course. But this inter-governmental body is of a much more recent time. The European Council did not acquire a President until 2009. Many nation states, with France at the helm, continue to try to transform Europe into a purely inter-governmental organisation led by the heads of state and government themselves. With a European Commission reduced to the role of secretariat. And a European Parliament to nod everything through. Regardless of whether the heads of state and government have time for this, or even whether they are capable of it, it is crystal clear what this would lead to: a sort of European board of directors. With a few large countries, above all France and Germany, running the show. Best to let them decide what is good or bad for Europe. Without taking account of the smaller Member States, let alone the interests of the European Citizens themselves.

To know how fatal this course would be, it is enough to remind oneself of the events of recent years. How in 2003 and 2005, Germany and France were themselves the first to breach the rules of Monetary Union without being punished, thereby undermining the credibility of the euro and the entire eurozone, whereas they are now hauling everybody over the coals. How in the last two years both countries have tried in vain to bring the euro crisis under control, but have each time failed because they have not been able to take anything more than half-hearted measures. When everybody knows that only a global and daring European vision can get us out of the mess. Neither the French President nor the German Chancellor has been able to represent Europe or speak in its name. They represent French and German interests respectively. Not the European interest. The speak on behalf of France and Germany respectively. Not on Europe's behalf. This can only be done by a democratic European Government placed under the direct control of representatives elected by all European citizens. Only the elected have European legitimacy. Not the French President appointed by a narrow majority of French men and women who bother to show up at Presidential elections. And not the German Chancellor either, who survives on the shaky confidence of a majority in the German Federal Parliament. In short, it is a flagrant lie to claim that the European Council has democratic legitimacy and the European Commission and European Parliament do not. Precisely the opposite is true.

4

We must not fall into the trap of national identity.
"National identity" is the latest manifestation of the
old nationalism. It is the latest disguise of nationalist
ideology. Used as a means of attacking multinational
and multicultural enemies all the harder: Europe
and the European Union in the first place. There is
not an inch of our body that believes that identity
does not exist or is not important. On the contrary.
It is the very being of each person. What we dispute
is not that you have it, but how others want to abuse
your identity. How they want to attach a "national"
label to it. How, in other words, they want to mould
that identity directly according to their own narrow
nationalistic view of society. Or even worse, that
want to use that identity to categorise and manipulate
society by pigeon-holing people.

Modern nationalistic ideology sounds very
simple. It is the modern, globalised world that
is the main enemy, the main culprit. It is a world
which turns at lightning speed and leaves people to
their fate without anything to hold on to, without
security. Fortunately there is identity, i.e. a sense of
belonging to a specific ethnic, religious or linguistic
community. It provides people with a beacon, an

anchor, a foothold with which to survive these uncertain and unstable times. Nationalistic ideology is based on the idea that identity is a shared and collective phenomenon that has the same impact on people of the same society. The only thing we have to do in life is to "discover" this unambiguous identity which is the same for everybody within the group.

The reality is different. There are as many identities as there are individuals. Each person is unique. And more importantly, everybody's identity is multi-faceted and not uniform as the nationalists would have us believe. There is a vast difference between the unambiguous identity with which nationalistic rhetoric is smeared and the multi-faceted identities which inhabit the real world. In Edinburgh, you're from Glasgow, in Manchester, you're Scottish, in Berlin, you're British, in America, you're European, in Lagos you're a white person. Your multi-faceted identity is a source of richness. A singular identity, on the contrary, is a straitjacket. Wanting to put a person into one category is to do him an injustice. To reduce him to an unwilling cog in a machine called society. A human being is much more than that. A human being inherits not only his individuality and personality. He also makes choices. He is creative. He makes decisions. He himself creates a large part of his identity and personality. Let us again stress that the quest for one shared "national" identity as a basis for organising society is a swindle, a form of intellectual piracy. It divides society up into a number of ethnic, national, cultural or religious "containers" or "bunkers" from which nobody can or may escape. Inevitably it leads to violence, to riots in your own neighbourhood, to hatred and war worldwide. The "murderous identity", as the Franco-Lebanese author Amin Maalouf called it. The twentieth century which has now ended, which was more murderous than ever, provided us with tragic evidence of this.

"Identity" means that people ascribe specific characteristics to a given group which are often radically different from those of somebody with a different identity. Differences separate. Somebody who is "different" is, in nationalist delusional thinking, only a small step from becoming an "enemy". "Identity" also leads to conformist behaviour, whereby one's critical thinking is switched off. One blindly follows traditions, even if they constitute direct discrimination against other races or the other sex. Eventually, indifference, hatred and violence towards "the others" is barely condemned. On the contrary, those who live with "the others" are regarded as "traitors" to their identity. After all, if mankind is reduced to its own group, noble principles such as law, tolerance or non-violence only apply within that group. It was "identity" which for so long kept Serbia from extraditing its war criminals. It was "identity" that led some Germans from protecting certain Nazis. For us, the future of Europe does not have the slightest thing to do with a quest for national identity(-ies). And the future certainly does not lie in a congress of national identities. A Europe of nation states is a relic of the past. Not a signpost to the future.

We should demand our "European passport". We must today dare to take an even more radical leap, a leap towards a fully fledged European nationality. We must no longer accept that the European nation states should want to confine each citizen, each subject within their own borders. Moreover, any discriminatory legislation that does just that should be banned outright or repealed. Why should it not be possible for people and families to have several nationalities? Why is it that children with parents of different nationalities are obliged at a certain moment in their lives to choose their nationality? Why prohibit or make it impossible for people to have dual or triple nationality? If a Pole in Amsterdam marries a Dutch person and his children speak Dutch and Polish fluently and probably English too, why oblige the children to choose between Dutch and Polish nationality? What has that got to do with anybody? Who in Heaven's name gains from this? Does Dutch society perhaps remain purer as a result? Does it help the Polish nation to retain its Polish nature? If one is born in Canada or the United States, it is perfectly possible to go through life with three or four passports. Why not in Europe?

Of course, if somebody wishes to identify with just one nationality, he should be perfectly able or entitled to do so. Just like a child of parents of different nationalities should have the opportunity and right to retain both nationalities. But is it not high time we introduced a European nationality and a European passport? Citizens should have the right to exchange their original nationality for European nationality or, if they wish, acquire European nationality in addition to their old nationality.

In short, let us complete what the European pioneers once began. Their efforts were enormous. Their vision a blessing. The results that have been achieved barely a half century later phenomenal. They united what it had never been possible to unite before. A generation of political leaders brought about what had seemed impossible in the previous thousand years. But the job is not done. A fully integrated and federal Europe is still far off. It is true that it has never happened anywhere in the world that sovereign states have transferred so much power to a supranational institution. But the increasing integration has come to a virtual standstill in the last ten years. Proposals to transfer further resources and powers are consistently swept off the table. Let us not bury our head in the sand. The European nation states are not in the slightest bit keen to transfer more powers. On the contrary, they are doing everything they can to apply the brakes. They shudder at the thought of a federal Europe. They sabotage any new step towards European unification. Above all, they fear losing power. And this without considering that they will no longer have any significance in tomorrow's world.

They do not understand that only a federal Europe will count in future. A federal Europe in which the Community institutions – the European Commission and the European Parliament – take the lead. A federal Europe with its own financial resources paid directly by the citizens. Not a Europe that must survive on not more than one per cent of European wealth, scraped together by the all too stingy Member States. A federal Europe that has sufficient resources to pursue a genuine policy. More efficient and cheaper due to economies of scale than the Member States can achieve separately. Not a Union that goes under at the first crisis as is now happening. But a federal Europe that draws up a sound political, economic, fiscal and budgetary policy. A Union that pursues an autonomous socio-economic and financial policy. And its own foreign policy based on a European diplomatic service and an autonomous European army. A European energy and industrial policy. A European home-affairs policy too, beginning with a unified asylum and migration policy. Finally, a political union which represents the European countries at global level. Because no individual Member State, however strong it may be, really counts today. Don't let yourself be fooled. In a world in which Americans and Russians, Chinese and Indians call the shots, only a united Europe can have any clout.

Ask not what Europe can do for you but what you can do for Europe. European unification is not entirely the work of politicians and bankers, but of countless Europeans who have given shape to the European project in word and deed. Often they have been men and women who were barely known, but who were nevertheless highly committed: writers, lawyers, civil servants, company managers, economists, scientists, teachers, culture vultures, historians, trade union representatives. Inspired men and women of all ages and all persuasions. People with an ideal. People with a belief. A belief in more Europe. A belief that they could also pass on to their political party or elected parliamentarians.

Enough of competition and centuries' old rivalries between nation states, resulting at best in one or other protectionist measure which invariably ended up costing the ordinary citizen. Enough too of exaggerated patriotic rhetoric. Enough of the false nationalist certainties which have served up two world wars and dozens of other violent conflicts. Enough of mutual blind hatred. Enough of the senseless bloodbaths. From now on it is together, as an association of Europeans, that we will tackle the problems. That we will rise to the challenges on our continent. That we will preserve our citizens' prosperity. That we will monitor peace and stability in the world. This is the job which previous generations handed to their elected representatives. And this is the job that must again be handed to the political class of today. The message that there is no nationalistic future for this continent. That the future of Europe will be post-national or no future at all.

The new generations must again be critical and uninhibited vis-à-vis their political leaders. At least like the generations before them. The generations that made Europe. Just like them, the new generations must hold their leaders to the

"European lesson". Prevent them from succumbing to the temptation of populism. Stop them from falling into the trap of nationalism. Temptations that are oh so great. Traps that are oh so deep. Because for a political leader there is nothing easier than to be swept away on a false tide of populism and nationalism. It's much easier than to row against it. Easier too than to convince public opinion of the need for the European project. Fortunately, in a democracy politicians must eventually stand for re-election. Must account for their deeds, their performance, their results, their successes and their failures. To be re-elected or finally disappear again into the masses. We must grasp the opportunity to finally be rid of all those who, for the sake of convenience, continue to fish in murky waters. We must use the power to put men and women at the helm who continue to believe firmly in the European future of this continent. And make no compromises in this respect. It is an "either/or" situation. Either we resolutely choose a federal Europe, a United States of Europe. Or we will fall back into our national oblivion.

Let us not fear what frightens us but fear fear itself. Knowledge neutralises fear. It is worse when we do not know. Then it is fear itself that takes the upper hand. The fear of fear, so to speak. Such fear usually causes a general feeling of unease and unsettles the whole of society. It might be fear of a serious natural disaster. Or of a devastating war. Or the fear for an unprecedented terrorist attack. Or a new epidemic,

64

such as AIDS in the 1980s, when the fear of an illness initially presented as only affecting homosexuals led to a wave of homophobia. It can be compared to the Black Death that killed thirty million people in Europe in just a few years in the middle of the 14th century. That is one in three Europeans. The plague did not disappear from Europe until the end of the 18th century, and it was only at the start of the 20th century that scientists were able to identify its origin: Koch's bacillus spread by rats at a time when nobody knew what a bacillus was. In the meantime, dozens, hundreds of "wizards", "Jews", "beggars", i.e. innocent people, had been killed in retribution for this terrible scourge. Times have changed.

Nowadays, the fear assumes a new face in a vague feeling of unease with the modern world. A globalised world which appears chaotic to many people. A world in which they apparently have too little to hold on to. A world too which is gradually reaching its "natural limits". Limits because the world's raw materials, and in particular fossil fuels, are finite and in short supply. Limits because the impending climate change, which is the consequence of our own way of living and working, will have particularly pernicious consequences. And this coupled with the glaring injustice that those who have had least to do with it are likely to be the ones who foot the bill.

What we must consider is that only Europe can provide an answer to this threat. That only Europe can remove the fear and the feeling of unease associated with it. After all, only Europe is in a position to gather the huge resources that are essential to convert our current society into the sustainable society of tomorrow. For the research and investments that this also requires. Only Europe can exhort or, if necessary, force the authorities of the other continents to make the same crucial choice. Only Europe can throw sufficient weight and influence into the debate.

We should be proud to be Europeans. Being European is your surname. Just like your own nationality is your first name. Nationality is what divides us. Europe, however, is what unites us. Each of us, our parents, our children, our forefathers and countless generations have contributed to today's Europe. Many languages and cultures, states and peoples, kings and emperors, monarchies and republics, religions and philosophies, inventors and discoverers, scientists and artists. Because the one thing Europe is not is a polished monolith. And it has never been one either. Europe has always been multi-faceted and not uniform. More of an idea than a continent. An idea with Celtic, Germanic and Romance roots. A world of Greek, Roman and Slavic saints and heroes. Fuelled by Jewish, Christian, Islamic and atheist sources of inspiration. European has never been able to tolerate an enforced uniformity. And Europe could certainly not put up with a straitjacketed discipline.

Europe is and remains a colourful beehive. And not a super-state in the making. This beehive must also continue to be the basis of a united and federal Europe. United in order to safeguard and nurture the multi-coloured European identity. Not in order to pick it up and place it under a bell jar. How are Europeans recognisable? Not so much by the colour of their skin, their nationality or their language, but more by the way of thinking and acting. The way they view people and things. Their way of life, seldom seen anywhere else in the world. Not even in the United States, where European immigrants became Americans.

A European feels passion for his town, has a strong attachment to his region, and loves his country without this preventing him from holding a deeply rooted European conviction. The "post-national" European identity is thus also nothing other than an extension of the layered personality we all possess. All those layers, all those different identities and personalities, can easily belong to one and the same individual without contradicting each other but without clashing with each other either.

Let us put European federalists at the helm. Politicians who only represent the European interest. There are enough national and regional parliaments for representatives who foster and defend national and regional interests to be elected to. The European Parliament must focus on the European interest, not the interests of the Member States. As voters, we should ensure that only politicians who actually champion the European cause are elected. Europe has no need for obstructionists who only bring Europe down. Those who stand waving their flags in the hemicycle as though possessed, while at the same time not having the slightest difficulty in pocketing an MEP salary. Even more so, Europe does not need "crooks" who use their European mandate to give the impression of being busy. Who draw a generous salary from Europe only to pursue purely national politics. Instead of sitting on committees or attending plenary sessions of the European Parliament, their only aim is to keep themselves free for re-election at national, regional or local level. We must therefore keep close track of our elected parliamentarians. Check whether they actually live up to their promise. Put them under pressure to think and act like a true European. In so doing, we should let our voices be heard. And above all, not leave them undisturbed for a single day. Because we should never forget that, for better or for worse, we too bear responsibility for the European project.

Time is running out for Europe. If we want the European project to remain on its feet, we have no time to waste. European democracy must shift to a higher gear immediately. The Parliament must map out the route and show the way, something which it is scarcely doing at the present time. It must also be ready to cross swords with the Member States. Not a single parliament in a single country in the world has been handed power in its lap. This has never happened. A parliament has to take power. Let us not be naïve. The old European nation states will never give up power without a fight. They will not spontaneously hand over power to a supra-national or federal Europe. This will have to be fought for.

This will require a struggle. Not with weapons, of course. But with arguments, with non-violent action and above all votes.

A clear victory for the pro-Europeans at the 2014 elections must herald the creation of a real constituent assembly. With the aim of establishing a truly federal Europe. A federal Europe which is no longer paralysed by the required unanimity of Member States, but a Europe that is governed by a real European Government, the successor to the present European Commission. A Europe led not by an accomplice of the Member States but a convinced federalist who breathes fresh life into the Commission's right of initiative. A leader who is directly elected by the people or at least by the European Parliament. A Europe that is subject to the democratic control and legitimacy of a Parliament that is only answerable to the citizens of Europe. Alongside a European Senate composed of representatives of the Member States. A Europe to which the citizens pay part of their taxes directly, putting an end to the shadowy funding we see today based on so-called national contributions which enable the Member States to hold the European Union in a crippling grip. It is the Member States who have an interest in keeping European finances shrouded in a thick mist without it being possible to determine how much money actually goes to Europe, why and what is to be done with it. The people of Europe have nothing to lose. Indeed they have everything to gain from greater transparency.

A Convention must therefore be convened immediately after the 2014 European elections with representatives and delegates from all sectors of European society. A Convention with only one goal in mind: the creation of a European federal Union. Let us compare it to the Philadelphia Convention of 1787 in the United States, when that country was transformed from a loose confederation of states into the strong federal association we see today.

It is now or never. European unification is ultimately not a purely European matter. It is also a global challenge. No other continent on this planet has ever seen or experienced a unification of this nature. Never before in the world have national states created a comparable supranational or federal authority. Until further notice, therefore, Europe is also our only means of entering the supranational or post-national world which is in the making. A world of continents and sub-continents and not of states. A world which wants to forge ahead without allowing itself to be intimidated too much by the past. A world which, in its turn, wishes to unite and not split up into even smaller entities. In brief, a world for the 21st and not the 19th century. Europe must determine the fate of the 21st century alongside America, China or India.

Europe must also give the economic and financial globalisation of today a social, ecological and political face. Europe must complete what it has begun at world level: globalisation. However, none of this can happen without one thing.

Europe must shake off its national demons once and for all. Europe must move on from the navel-gazing of its nation states for good. A radical shift is truly needed in Europe. A genuine revolution. A European federal Union must be established. A federal Union which allows Europe to take its place in the forthcoming post-national world as quickly as possible. The heads of state and government who do not realise this are cowardly, lazy and short-sighted. Let us shake them from their inertia. Hold a mirror up to their powerlessness. Not leave them alone for a single day. Let us go forwards to the other Europe, the Europe of the future.

Daniel Cohn-Bendit
and Guy Verhofstadt

INTERVIEW

By Jean Quatremer

(Journalist at Libération, author of the blog
Coulisses de Bruxelles – Brussels Backstage)

THE TEMPTATION
OF NATIONAL RETRENCHMENT

JEAN QUATREMER: *Is your manifesto for a postnational Europe not completely out of step with the current thinking in States which seem more tempted by national retrenchment, given the economic crisis?*

DANIEL COHN-BENDIT: It's true, we are risking preaching in the ideological wilderness. But we wanted to give a possible vision of the future of Europe, that is, of a postnational federation, as we are convinced that we have reached a time in history when the nation State has run its course. Today, no-one knows where we are headed any longer, which explains the rise in Euroscepticism; the European aircraft is on automatic pilot, but it does not have a specific destination.

JQ: *There is the feeling above all that the aircraft has landed in the middle of nowhere.*

DCB: That's true, but it must take off again to reach somewhere. Europe has progressed considerably during the last fifty years, but faced with the economic crisis, it has shown its limits. Now, it is all or nothing: either we draw a veil over it, as we cannot remain in this state of lethal incompleteness permanently. Or, Europe is necessary to cope with the crisis and globalisation, so the choice of federalism must clearly be made.

75

It is not a question of campaigning for a federal "revolution" which will not happen, but of starting a process that will take us there.

GUY VERHOFSTADT: Nowadays, we no longer dare to have a radical vision of the future. What is the choice offered by the political parties to European public opinion? Either Euroscepticism, on the pretext that the Union is not functioning well, or the defence of what exists, whereas it is the imbalances of Europe today that are behind the current crisis. The people must be given another choice, which is what we are doing with our manifesto. Make no mistake: we are criticising Europe as it is at present as radically as the Eurosceptics, but our conclusion is radically different.

JQ: *Today, the Federalists have almost disappeared as a political force …*

DCB: Twenty or thirty years ago, the idea of federalism was abstract. It was above all about being "together" so that there would no longer be war. Today, with enlargement, globalisation and the financial crisis, federalism has become much more concrete. It is therefore not so easy to call oneself a "federalist".

GV: That is quite right. Up to now, federalism was understood to be a process for getting rid of obstacles (to freedom of movement, trade etc.) and a way of overcoming history.

Now, it is a case of sharing concrete policies which, up to now, were at the heart of States' sovereignty: social issues, tax, the economy, the budget, defence, foreign policy.

DCB: Europe is still essentially an area of nation States which are trying to come together, with difficulty. However, this process is too slow, given the issues at stake. We therefore propose to reinvent the federal idea, bring it back to life. It is not easy, as we have no historical precedent to rely on.

JQ: *Is the decline of the idea of federalism not also a British victory, as they have always been allergic to it? It was the United Kingdom which, in 1991, during the negotiation of the Maastricht Treaty, succeeded in making the "f word" permanently taboo...*

GV: Yes indeed, London succeeded in reducing the European Union to its single dimension of the "internal market", outside the single currency of course, for which London obtained an "opt out". Just as the euro came into force, I remember very clearly – I was Prime Minister of Belgium at the time – discussions on the common economic policy which was to accompany the single currency. This was summarised in the famous "Lisbon strategy" (adopted in 2000) which aimed to "co-ordinate" national efforts with a view to making Europe into the "most competitive economy in the world" by 2010.

DCB: At that time, the States refused to accept any constraints, any common policy. They would merely take as an example the "best practices" of others, without any obligation, without any power of control being given to the Commission. We can see the results: it has been an overwhelming failure.

JQ: *Was it therefore after the adoption of the Maastricht Treaty, in December 1991, that any political vision of Europe was abandoned in favour of a purely mercantile vision?*

GV: If there is a benefit to the crisis that we are suffering, it is that it shows the limits of this approach. It is proof that Europe, or at least the euro zone, cannot operate without a common budgetary, fiscal, economic and social policy.

DCB: After Maastricht, we moved into another era. Europe was faced simultaneously with the challenge of globalisation, the war in the Balkans, the climate crisis, and the financial and economic crisis. Governments were paralysed by this, and have gradually withdrawn into their own national domain instead of developing the construction of the Community which would have enabled them to meet all these challenges.

GV: The disappearance of the Soviet threat in 1990 played a fundamental role in this national retrenchment. It was as if the Europeans thought that the need for a conscience, a spirit, a European response had disappeared. It was in a way the "end of the story". From that moment on, it was thought that simply coordination between the national States would be more than sufficient. The last major project was the euro, a project supported by the French President François Mitterrand and the German Chancellor Helmut Kohl. If the single currency had not been decided in 1991, it would never have happened, I am convinced of it. Berlin and Paris knew they had to seize a historic moment.

DCB: It is true that the idea of Europe was to avoid one country dominating the old continent again, but it was also to provide a pole of stability against Communism. When the USSR collapsed and German unification took place, the question of dominance, which it was thought had been dealt with, arose again with the reappearance of a large Germany in the centre of the continent. That is why the single currency was launched, to anchor Germany finally in Europe and avoid its being tempted by a "Sonderweg", a solitary path fraught with danger. We exchanged German unification for European development. Without this political constraint, Guy is right, the euro would never have seen the light of day. This was a phenomenal leap of integration, but the governments were not capable of thinking through the consequences.

JQ: *The idea was that the advent of the single currency would cause a "federal impact"....*

DCB: This is an example of infantile historical determinism. It is astonishing that politicians can believe that history is made automatically.

GV: There are always political decisions to be made, decisions which involve risks for those who take them. As was feared, no decision was taken; the politicians chose the option of the lowest immediate cost, leaving it to their successors to pay the bill for their lack of action.

JQ: *The geopolitical aim of the Euro perhaps outweighed any other consideration...*

DCB: Absolutely. The sacrifice of the Deutsche mark was far from being meaningless as it was one of the elements comprising post-war German identity.
There were two major events that enabled Germany to acquire a new identity, without the horrors of Nazism, and to return to the civilised world. The first was the German victory in the 1954 World Cup, nine years after the end of the war, which meant that the world could talk about Germany other than in terms of a conquered country responsible for one of the greatest massacres in history. The second was the affirmation of its economic strength, free of any political ambition, seen in a strong and stable deutsche mark. The mark was the European currency par excellence, the absolute reference point. Nothing like the franc, which was a devalued currency to which the French were not particularly attached.

GV: It is clearly because the introduction of the single currency was first and foremost a geopolitical decision that the progress that should have accompanied it at the economic, fiscal, social and institutional level was not made. It all happened as if the decision itself had exhausted the Member States. A comparison with the United States is illuminating: they began by creating a political union around 1785-87. Then, two years later, they set up a Treasury; then after two years they introduced Treasury certificates; and two years after that they laid the foundations of what would become the dollar. We launched the euro because of time pressures while there was absolutely no agreement on the need to create a political union!

DCB: The emergence of the United States followed the American revolution and the American States did not in any way resemble the nation States that constitute Europe. Our historical process is the other way round.

GV: I only make this comparison to show the path we still have to follow. The launch of the euro was the right geopolitical choice to make at that time, I do not question that at all. But, now we must use the momentum of the crisis to achieve political union. It is clear what must be done and the markets have known it for a long time: we must build a European State. While States can exist without their own currency, a currency cannot exist without a State. We must have a clearly identified authority that can

81

create confidence on the markets and ensure that investors who have provided loans will get their money back.

DCB: I totally agree. The euro was rightly seen as something that would galvanise Europe and that is why all the States, except for Great Britain and Sweden, wanted to be part of it. An authority means sovereignty. An economic sovereignty which implies political sovereignty. And political sovereignty only exists if there is economic and financial sovereignty. Now, we must look at how to organise this sovereignty. Federalism is the only possible answer for Europe. A centralised State like France cannot be envisaged.

DOES EUROPE STILL HAVE A RAISON D'ETRE?

JQ: *Is it not the case that one of the reasons for the dissatisfaction of public opinion as regards the Community structure is that much was promised and these promises have not materialised? For example, it was claimed that the single market would create millions of jobs, that the euro would prevent investors from attacking any country and would ensure our prosperity, etc.*

GV: We must not throw the baby out with the bath water! Because the single market has created millions of jobs: without it, unemployment would have been much higher. We must not pretend that the economic situation had not changed at the same time as the acceleration of globalisation. In 1985, when the completion of the internal market was launched, China, India or Brazil were not yet our competitors. Unemployment in the Union, both due to the single market and the single currency, greatly decreased up to the start of the financial crisis, in 2007-2008. In the same way, the euro ensured stability for ten years, eliminating exchange crises between the countries in the euro zone; you will recall the consequences of the monetary crises of 1992-1995! We also enjoyed very low interest rates to finance our debts, true European bonds before the term was invented. Finally the single currency enabled us to cope with the financial crisis which came from the United States, a crisis which has devastated the whole planet. If we had not had the euro, it would have been a catastrophe with a spate of devaluations, a rise in inflation, the return of protectionism, etc. It is not for nothing that Iceland asked to join the Union.

But it is true that in 1999, when the single currency was launched, we under-estimated its structural weaknesses. In particular, the cheap financing of our debts weakened, in some countries, the will to see through reforms to maintain their competitiveness. This is a danger which now weighs heavily on several countries in the euro zone, including Germany where the short term financing rates (six months) are negative; they receive money to borrow it! I recall that the German public debt, in particular, is more than 80% of GDP, however, which does not justify such rates.

DCB: We have to beware of misinterpretations: this debt is largely due to funding unification, as West Germany invested to a huge extent in the East to bring the former RDA out of the misery into which Communism had plunged it. To answer your question, I believe that it is still difficult when one is coming out of one era and entering another. You are obliged to some extent to give an idyllic view of what will happen...

JQ: *One of the arguments put forward most frequently to justify the existence of Europe is that it has guaranteed peace in the old continent. But more and more voices are being heard saying that peace is due above all to the American military presence...*

DCB: The Americans were there not to make peace in Europe, but to make Europe into a bastion against Communism, which ended up with the creation of NATO. The United States, with NATO, guaranteed peace with the USSR, that is true. But the process of Community integration took place in parallel, without being directly linked to it. Europe was set up after its third civil war (1870, 1914-18, and 1939-1945), as its people wanted no more wars. It was not the American policeman who imposed anything, otherwise I would have to explain how the Americans played a role in the construction of the Community, which is the last thing I would do. The process of integration was based, in particular, on Franco-German reconciliation. It is amusing to think it probably happened with a major misunderstanding: for General De Gaulle, it was a case of creating a counterweight to the United States, for Konrad Adenauer it was to anchor Germany to the west to avoid it moving between east and west, which was what led to two world wars...

GV: If it were sufficient to have a worldwide police force, there would have been worldwide peace since 1945... Seriously, the Europeans learned totally different lessons following the two world wars, while in both cases the Americans were involved. After the First World War, it was thought that mono-ethnic and mono-cultural states would put an end to the question of nationalities, which drive conflicts. The result was to create the conditions for the Second World War. After the Second World War, it was decided, on the contrary, to overcome the warmongering nation States by creating the Union. But this was not a foregone conclusion: therefore in 1954, in the Cold War, France buried the notion of European defence, which shows that the American presence absolutely did not guarantee the construction of the Community.

DCB: The American attitude as regards Germany following the war is an interesting one.

There were two options on the table. Either the country would be divided and there would be an industrial desert so that the Germans would not recover. That was the Morgenthau plan. Or Germany (and the Europeans) would be allowed to rebuild, to set up a democratic defence against Communism. That was the Marshall plan, which was finally implemented to the benefit of all of Western Europe. In 1950, in particular, the German debt was frozen until the signature of a peace treaty between the allies so that there was no repetition of the mistake of the Treaty of Versailles which brought Germany to its knees. That was also why Helmut Kohl did not want a peace treaty to be a prior condition of German unification. His argument was that the charge for the debt added to that of unification would have been too great a burden.

JQ: *I wonder what the result of a referendum on Franco-German reconciliation or the freezing of the German debt would have been in 1950...*

GV: That is clear proof that politicians must not always follow the public opinion of the time. They must have a vision and try to convince the people that it is the right one.

DCB: We must learn lessons from the past. While it is true that some countries have been irresponsible in managing their public finances, they must be given time to reform, like the Germans had in 1950.

JQ: *If the European people no longer want war, does Europe still have a raison d'être?*

DCB: We should ask the question in a different way: can a State deal with globalisation or the crises we now face on its own? For us, the answer is no. We must remember that in 25 years' time, no European State, not even Germany, will be part of the G8 grouping together the main world powers. We will no longer have any influence, will be in isolation and disappear one by one, and our social model would not survive. The national political elites do not dare face up to this question and tell their people. Europe is not an ideological question, it is all about survival!

GV: It is not that the nation State is the absolute evil and it must be destroyed. Its creation in the 18th century was part of progress which brought together, within one geopolitical area, regions, towns and villages. It increased well-being and allowed the development of democracy. But now we are entering a new era, that of globalisation. The balance of power will from now on be seen at subcontinental or continental level. It is at that level that the unity will be achieved which will enable us to progress economically and defend our interests before the rest of the world.

"DEGLOBALISE" OR PUT PRESSURE ON GLOBALISATION?

JQ: *Some politicians, of the radical right or left, such as the socialist Arnaud Montebourg in France, propose "deglobalising"…*

GV: How can one "deglobalise"? As there is no question of convincing China to go back to its state of under-development, I imagine that this would mean European or national protectionism? But this would not work as we are all interconnected, you cannot go back unless there is a worldwide disaster. If we were to protect an industry, we would be exposed to reprisals on a sector that may be vital for us. This does not mean that free trade as it exists is satisfactory and that I am happy with it; there should be more regulation, minimum standards, particularly social and environmental standards. But it is through Europe that we will succeed in imposing them within the World Trade Organisation (WTO), by negotiation and not starting trade wars. In any case, it is not France or Germany alone which will do this, as they do not carry much weight in world terms, compared with the giants of the United States, China, Brazil and India.

DCB: When Nicolas Sarkozy said that Europe must protect, he was not wrong. Let us look at the case of the Chinese solar panels produced at low cost and which threaten European businesses, particularly in

Germany. It is up to Europe and not any one country to impose free and undistorted competition upon the Chinese. In other words, force them to comply with social standards, including the freedom to form trade unions, as well as environmental standards, as it alone has the clout to do so.

JQ: *But the Union has taken no action...*

DCB: It is a matter of political will. The Americans have imposed a tax on Chinese solar panels. If Europe does not decide on reprisals, it is because the Commission and the governments do not wish to do anything for ideological reasons.

GV: One can also be offensive and not only defensive. If Europe had more budgetary resources, it could launch a major research programme on solar cells which would enable us to take back control of the situation.

DCB: The drama of Europe is that it does not dare to use its power. For example, it is absurd that each State is fighting its own corner against tax havens instead of giving that task to the Union. If the Union were to put pressure on Switzerland, a tax haven at the heart of Europe, as the United States has, the balance of power would be different. It would be sufficient to tell Switzerland that if the question of the exchange of information is not regulated, its banks will no longer be able to have access to the European area. Believe me, the question would be settled quickly! Instead of which, Berlin, Paris, or Rome each negotiate their own corner, trying to obtain a national advantage instead of thinking of the general European interest.

JQ: *Trade defence measures are decided by simple majority by the Commission, which has one Commissioner per Member State. It is easy to imagine that a coalition of small trading nations may block them to the detriment of the major industrial powers. Therefore trade defence measures cannot be dealt with in themselves, there is also an institutional problem.*

GV: It is never the case that the large countries are on one side and the small countries are on the other. It is more of an ideological problem: there are those who are for setting in place minimum ecological and social criteria and those who are against. This is the case within the Commission, and within the Council of Ministers.

JQ: *That is certainly so, but in the meantime, no trade defence measures can be decided whereas this can be done at the level of each country. The fact that the majority of countries and European managers are fiercely in favour of free trade blocks the States which are less in favour.*

DCB: That is true. Only national protection measures would be of no use because France itself would not withstand the impact. Coping with Chinese, Indian or American reprisals alone is not the same thing as coping with them on a continental level. Chris Patten, the former European Commissioner for Foreign Trade, said that the Chinese only understood the balance of power. They need us as much as we need them. We should stop allowing them to slice us up like they do at the moment, because the Germans want to send them their cars, the French their TGVs with a nuclear power plant as well, etc.

It is true that each country has its own economic-political culture and that each one can feel bullied by the others. But it is possible to convince the other States, to topple the ideological majorities as can be seen in the response by Europeans to the euro zone crisis. The decisions taken would have been unimaginable five or six years ago, whether it concerned the financial solidarity between the States in the euro zone, European banking supervision, budgetary union etc.

GV: I remember that in 2008, there was absolutely no question of European banking union. Angela Merkel, the German chancellor, thought then that the regulation of the banks was exclusively a national responsibility.

THE EURO ZONE
IN POLITICAL CRISIS

JQ: *Nevertheless, it needed the battering of the crises, which put millions of Europeans into poverty, for the Union, that is the Community institutions and governments, to abandon its ideology of laissez-faire and self-regulation, and even then with some difficulty.*

DCB: What is important is that Europe is in a position to decide. That is why Guy and I are fighting for it. Three years ago, Garry Kasparov introduced me to his friend Edward Limonov, an ultra-nationalist, and he said to me: "If we have a parliament resulting from free elections in Russia tomorrow, Limonov will be on the other side of the hemi-cycle, but today we are fighting together because we both want a free parliament in Russia." It is the same for Europe: Guy and I are not on the same side politically, but we are fighting together to achieve a European political area where we can express ourselves fully. Then it is a question of a balance of political power. We may have at European level a neo-liberal or socialist majority, exactly as in each country. It is up to the political parties to tell us what their idea of the market is and up to European citizens to vote for majorities who will decide the political direction of the Union. Nothing is decided in advance.

GV: The global financial crisis has proved to us to what extent the nation State is no longer suited to the modern world. While the markets have become globalised, political organisation has hardly changed since the end of the 19th Century and remains based on the nation. There is therefore a considerable imbalance in favour of the markets which act very quickly without being hindered by borders, whereas States must coordinate, with some difficulty, in order to deal with the situation, to find a compromise which is very often not enough as the markets have moved on in the meantime. The result is that it is the markets which impose their rhythm and will upon the States. It is essential to restore the balance between finance and politics and for Europe, this must be by means of a true federation capable of reacting quickly without going through the nation States.

JQ: *In other words, the crisis in the euro zone is also a crisis in political governance as the States failed to adopt instruments that would have enabled them to avoid it (budgetary, banking and fiscal union, European bonds, European democracy, etc.). In a way, the Union stopped in midstream after creating the single currency and it was surprised by the water rising so suddenly...*

GV: Exactly. You have to go back to the beginning of the debt crisis to understand what happened. At the end of 2009, the European Central Bank announced that, in the near future, it would no longer accept guarantees (collateral) with a rating less than A-in exchange for its loans and no longer BBB+ as it had done since 2007 in order to provide liquidity to the commercial banks which were no longer able to obtain financing from other banks. This strategy for coming out of the banking crisis in fact became a strategy for entering the debt crisis. As it was at that moment that the financial institutions began to get rid of the Greek securities which would soon no longer be eligible under guarantee, as the rating agencies had downgraded Greece substantially at the end of 2009-beginning of 2010 placing its debt in the speculative investment grade. It was at that moment that the Heads of State and of governments lacked courage, they were even cowards. If they had stated their solidarity with Greece and guaranteed its debts because the euro zone is a monetary and economic union, the crisis would not even have begun. A simple sentence would have sufficed, but they did not say it, which sowed doubts concerning solidity within the euro zone; a union without solidarity is not a union! Then, the States organised about twenty summits, but each time they were content to come up with half-measures hoping that they would be enough, which was not the case.

If the crisis is still going on and is devastating the economies in the euro zone, it is because the governments do not want to admit that the crisis is a political one and requires political solutions, that is greater integration. Fortunately, it seems, since the European Council of 28 and 29 June 2012, that they are beginning to stop denying the truth: they have started work leading to a banking union and have asked the Presidents of the Commission, the European Council, the Eurogroup and the ECB to prepare a road map setting out in detail the path towards greater political integration.

JQ: *We should not hide the particular responsibility of Germany in making the crisis worse. I would remind you that in December 2008, the first tensions over the debt of the peripheral States of the euro zone arose. But Peer Steinbrück, the German Finance Minister, following secret negotiations with Christine Lagarde, the French Finance Minister, Jean-Claude Juncker, the President of the Eurogroup, and Jean-Claude Trichet, the President of the ECB, stated in February 2009 that the euro zone would support countries in difficulty. This was sufficient to reassure the markets. But in December 2009, Angela Merkel was in coalition with the Liberals of the FDP, and the tone changed. The new majority hesitated to support Greece whereas the grand coalition had not prevaricated. As the entourage of Nicolas Sarkozy said, "for two years, we have tried to stop Angela Merkel from jumping ship" because she was ready to leave the euro. This crisis is certainly political, but it was made worse by Germany which has lost its European principles.*

DCB: You are not alone in thinking that. Helmut Kohl, the former Christian Democrat German Chancellor, exclaimed in 2011, according to several German newspapers, "she's breaking up my Europe".

The ecologist Joschka Fischer, former Foreign Minister, published an article at the beginning of June 2012 which violently attacked the Chancellor's policy. I quote: "Do we Germans understand our pan-European responsibility? It certainly does not appear so. In fact, Germany has rarely been as isolated as it is today. Almost no-one understands our dogmatic austerity policy, which goes against past experience, and we are thought to be going in the wrong direction or definitely against the tide." He ends with this warning: "Germany destroyed itself – and the European order – twice in the 20th century, but then convinced the West that it had learned from its past mistakes. It was only in that way – reflected most vividly in its joining the European project – that Germany obtained consent for its reunification. It would be both tragic and ironic if a restored Germany, by peaceful means and with the best of intentions, brought about the ruin of the European order a third time." You could not express it any more clearly.

GV: If the euro were to disappear, the country that would suffer most would be Germany. It would see its currency appreciate greatly compared with that of its partners and would lose a large part of its export markets. Some studies estimate that the impact would be three times the effect of the bankruptcy of Lehman Brothers in September 2008. It is unimaginable!

DCB: It is true that the German government is seriously reeling, but its strategy is now fixed: it wants to save the euro, because German interest depends on it. But for the Chancellor, the single currency can only function if German financial and economic culture becomes European culture. In particular, she is demanding that the countries in the euro zone implement austerity policies to re-establish their public finances.

She refuses to consider that a strategy of investment, which would accompany the necessary structural reforms to put the economies back on the rails, would boost growth which would have a beneficial effect on budgetary equilibrium. A rescue package that exclusively involves an austerity policy strangles the driving productive forces of a country. The example of the policy of the Spanish Prime Minister Mr Rajoy has shown this perfectly. It is an ideological problem which is blocking and deconstructing Europe. Mario Monti, the Italian Prime Minister, may manage to break down this barrier; he is in the process of proving that structural reforms alone are not enough to restart the economic machine and that the strategy for coming out of the crisis has to include a stimulus.

GV: Italy is a very good example showing that the dogma of budgetary discipline alone is just as ineffective in providing a way out of the crisis as a stimulus through public expenditure alone. Mario Monti is carrying out reforms, but as solidarity is not organised in the euro zone, he is still faced with interest rates of between 5 and 7%, which is untenable in the medium term. The consequence of these high rates: around half of Italy's efforts will be used to remunerate international investors! Solidarity must therefore be organised within the euro zone, by mutualising national debts, at least partially, allowing interest rates to fall substantially. By refusing this mutualisation, the choice is to favour shareholders, those whom Angela Merkel wanted to make pay at the beginning of the crisis…this is another inconsistency, you have to admit it. Because with the European Financial Stability Facility (EFSF) and the European Stability Mechanism (ESM), funds which do not solve the problem structurally and which are supposed to avoid debt mutualisation, the choice has been made to charge the German taxpayer, whom the Chancellor rightly wants to protect!

JQ: *How can we ask France or Germany to bail out Italian, Spanish or Greek expenditure while they have no control over the governments of those countries? This is a real problem of democracy: if the citizens of a country want to overthrow their government because they are not happy with how they run the country, there is no question of giving this power to all the citizens of the euro zone. Tomorrow, I would not like to have to reimburse the amount that Antonis Samaras may spend buying American tanks. Financial solidarity is not viable without political responsibility.*

DCB: But the point is, Greece has not bought American tanks, it has purchased frigates and submarines from Germany and France! As long as it got into debt to keep French and German companies in business, it was not much of a problem. When the euro zone loaned money to Greece in April 2010, Angela Merkel and Nicolas Sarkozy did point out to the Papandreou government that the contracts with French and German arms companies had to be fulfilled. The problem is therefore more complex. But it is still true that solidarity implies political control.

In particular, it is essential that the European Commission, which is now in charge of controlling national budgets, is no longer an assembly of technocrats who are not accountable, but a political government subject to the control of the European Parliament and the Council of Ministers. That being so, I recognise that I am not fully answering your question: how can European citizens be truly concerned with what happens in Greece?

THE STATES RESPONSIBLE FOR WORSENING THE CRISIS

JQ: *The euro zone crisis has shown that a single currency cannot function permanently with seventeen sovereign economic and budgetary policies, but no government is stating clearly what it wants for the future. Mario Draghi, the President of the ECB, has called upon them to meet their responsibilities, as it is not up to a central bank to take political decisions.*

DCB: Since the beginning of the crisis, the European Central Bank (ECB) has not looked at the European treaties before acting. Also, lawyers are still wondering if it has the right to buy State bonds on the secondary market, that is resale, so as to lower interest rates. And if the euro is truly threatened, I am sure that it will go even further. It is already acting like a federal bank and has prepared the ground to lead us towards the creation of a European Treasury which will issue Euro-bonds.

GV: But, while the ECB went beyond its mission as defined by the Treaties, it announced that, from now on, it would not do any more while the States have not taken the necessary steps towards more federalism.

DCB: It is for that reason that we are publishing this manifesto: it is time for politicians to open the debate on the Europe they want. Or rather on the type of

Europe we absolutely need to find a way out of the crises we are experiencing. In other words, it is no longer the time for prevarication over the Europe we would like to see but rather on the Europe that has become necessary.

GV: The problem is that politicians are first and foremost responsible to their national public opinion and not to all European citizens. They think "local" before thinking "continent". We want to explain to them that national and European interest are one and the same and that the European interest determines the protection of national interests.

JQ: *Occasionally we wonder whether the politicians have the necessary theoretical instruments to develop European thought. Thus, Nicolas Sarkozy, during the 2012 presidential campaign, argued for an "intergovernmental federation", two terms that were mutually incompatible. It is like wishing for rainy sunshine, or sunny rain...*

DCB: That goes back a long way. Before him, Jacques Delors had spoken about the "federation of nation States" to avoid the word federalism...It is a shame. We must recognise that the European resilience of the post-war period is no longer there. Nicolas Sarkozy admitted that France did not have much influence in the world without Europe, but it is difficult for a French president to recognise it, as it takes away much of his function. His "intergovernmental federation", is in fact a way of creating a Franco-German board of Europe, consisting of the two big players, and of maintaining the idea that France, and therefore its president, still count for something ...

GV: But Berlin and Paris have failed miserably in their management of the euro zone crisis. The European Council of Heads of State and government has proved to be unable to adopt anything other than half-measures which solve nothing. Within such an enclosed area, we cannot get past the national level. The "Heads" do not see that adding together the national interests does not always equal the European interest. It is at European level, at federal level, that action must be taken.

DCB: This idea of "intergovernmental federalism" must have occurred to Nicolas Sarkozy when he held the rotating presidency of the EU, in the second half of 2008, When the conflict in Georgia arose, the French head of State, President of the Council, leapt into his aircraft, negotiated with Putin and Medvedev and managed to convince them not to invade that country. It was a moment of extreme pleasure for him, of omnipotence – French President and European President, that's the future!

GV: While it worked in Georgia, it did not for the euro zone crisis. Germany firstly wanted to allow Greece to go bankrupt and even at one point argued for it to leave the euro. Finally, it was convinced by France to support it. Then the Franco-German agreement of Deauville, in October 2010, which stated that the debts of States in the euro zone could be restructured in future, led to a new panic which forced Ireland and then Portugal to ask for aid. As if that were not enough, they lit the fire again in July 2011 by deciding to restructure the Greek debt. On each occasion, Berlin and Paris concluded intergovernmental agreements which consisted of joining their interests to one another. But this does not represent the interest of Europe. The interest of Europe is higher and different from that of Germany or France. Saving the banks in Europe is different from saving French or German banks.

JQ: *In other words, you do not settle a financial crises by means of diplomatic compromises.*

GV: Exactly. No-one denies now that without political, fiscal and economic union, monetary union cannot last. There is no example in the world or in history of a currency existing without a State. But governments preferred patchwork solutions to an openly federal approach which would have allowed the crisis to be resolved globally. The European federation will perhaps see the light of day, but it will be against the will of many politicians.

DCB: But it is no longer the time for prevarication. The worsening of the crisis means we must make a choice quickly.

GV: Why was a single market in Europe not created after the First World War, which would have avoided many problems? Because at the time, the idea of the nation State was so strong that no-one could imagine overcoming it. It needed the total defeat of Europe in 1945 for people to start thinking differently.

JQ: *In fact, we had to wait for the Franco-British crisis in Suez in 1956 for France to become aware that it was no longer a major world player. Under the joint pressure of the Americans and the Soviets, London and Paris had to evacuate Egypt which they had invaded following the nationalisation of the Suez canal. At that time, Great Britain chose an unconditional alignment with the United States while France bet on Europe to find room for manoeuvre. It was not by chance that the Treaty of Rome was signed the following year. We therefore had to wait more than ten years after the Second World War for the Community adventure to be truly begun.*

DCB: In that time between 1945 and 1957, there were political personalities like Jean Monnet, Robert Schuman or even Altiero Spinelli who dared to imagine a new organisation of States in Europe which would lead to federalism. Their thinking was against the majority. It is what we want to do at our level. We want to challenge the European political classes by proposing a new project that can move Europe out of the crises it is currently facing. Of course, I can already hear the critics: all of that is fine, but it is too radical, it isn't possible.

The alternative is simple, however: either we continue to do what we have done, that is Europe in small steps, by trial and error, small compromises and every day we are losing public opinion more and more. Or we define a much more radical vision to give the people a political perspective.

I am not saying that Europe is in itself a miracle cure, but I defend the idea that without Europe we will not come out of the current crisis, as it is a big enough political area to have an influence on world affairs. Obviously this does not mean the disappearance of the political debate on, for example, whether or not there should be a social policy, tax harmonisation, protectionism etc. When Marx asked the question of bourgeois revolution, he considered that it was a necessary historical step to allow proletarian revolution.
For him, it was a historical process. This reasoning can be applied perfectly to the construction of the Community.

JQ: *Is Euroscepticism therefore reactionary?*

DCB: Absolutely. Euroscepticism is reactionary and damaging for citizens, because the Eurosceptics want to leave the citizens without protection.

GV: The Eurosceptics want us to go back to the system of nation States, whose failure in Europe is clear. We want to fight against this false idea that only the nation State can protect us in the globalised world of tomorrow whereas that is not the case, whether it is socially, environmentally or commercially etc. The world will be organised from now on around poles which can be described as empires, with all the precautions that word implies: the United States, China or even India, these are Empires, not nation States. The Indian sub-continent is a good example of what must be done. It is a geographical area where dozens of ethnic groups speaking dozens of languages and practising a multitude of religions live together. However, it is indisputable that it forms a single entity and even a democratic entity.

JQ: *But Europe is not an empire.*

GV: That is the problem! Europe must become an "empire" in the good sense of the word, that is a continental pole able to include, on a voluntary basis, different nations, ethnic groups, cultures or religions. But we are suffering from having invented nation States and the nationalism that goes with them in the 18th Century and we are having trouble getting past them. The euro zone crisis will perhaps force us to move, however. It is only under constraint that things change.

JQ: *Why did you not launch your manifesto ten years ago?*

GV: Crises create opportunities. When everything is going well, you have the impression that it will go on forever. So, at the beginning of the 21st Century, the European economy was growing strongly and it was thought that with the Lisbon Strategy the most competitive economy in the world would be created by 2010. Almost all those in charge thought that the architecture of the euro zone was satisfactory and we could continue along those lines. It was only in the crisis that we could see the limits of the system. Now, very few people still think that an economic and budgetary union is not necessary. Politicians do not take the necessary steps unless their backs are to the wall.

JQ: *In 2006, when you were still Prime Minister of Belgium, you published a book proposing the creation of the "United States of Europe".*

GV: Ah, that created a great scandal in the European Council. Some of my colleagues asked me if I was completely mad... I wrote it in reaction to the failure of the European Constitutional Treaty in 2005.

JQ: *But at the time of the Treaty of Nice in 2000, whose failure was the origin of the European Constitutional Treaty, you were not yet a federalist!*

GV: But in Belgium one is naturally a federalist!

JQ: *I saw you arrive in Nice defending Belgian interests. You became a federalist during the four days of debates at daggers drawn between the States which ended up with the worst Treaty ever drawn up.*

GV: It is true that I began the debate in Nice on the question of the equality of voting rights in the Council of Ministers between Belgium and the Netherlands, which could be taken as defending Belgian national interests. But if one were to upset the equality which existed up to that point between our two countries, I think it would have had to be the same between France and Germany. You cannot say there are two categories of States, the large States which are equal and the others which saw their influence in the Council depend on their population. It was a way of saying that there was a sort of European Board of the major countries. This unremitting defence of national interests made me think. All the more so, as it is the only summit I know that recognised, when the work was completed, that the Treaty was not satisfactory and the work had to start again as quickly as possible. It was in Nice that it was decided to launch the convention which was to draw up the European Constitutional Treaty, which unfortunately failed.

DCB: I think that anyone who exercises power becomes intergovernmental. It is the hard drive of national politicians. To blame them for it would be absurd. It is the influence of the Council in European decisions that must be called into question. Whether there is a European Senate or the governments defend the interest of their national area, as is the case in the American Senate or the Bundesrat, it is quite normal. The problem is finding a balance between this legislative institution and those who defend the general European interest, that is the European Parliament and the Commission.

Guy and I are Members of the Parliament, and that is why we have written this manifesto, to influence the future. The best way of doing it is to do it between two people who are not of the same political family in any way, otherwise it would have been too easy. We do not always have the same opinions on the policies to be followed, but we always reach decisions backed up by a particular vision of Europe.

COMMUNITY INSTITUTIONS DRIFTING OUT OF CONTROL

JQ: *Governments are always being accused, but there is one major absentee over the past fifteen years, the European Commission*

DCB: That's correct. The Commission has a monopoly on the legislative initiative, a determining power. It could therefore put a proposal on the table on debt mutualisation , for example. But it does not.

JQ: *It did draw up a Green Paper on the subject at the end of 2011.*

GV: If you don't want to make a decision, you draw up a Green Paper. Why did it not lodge a legislative proposal for the creation of a redemption fund for national debts that exceed 60% of the GDP or a variant? That would have a beneficial effect on the markets and the States that are opposed to it would have much more difficulty in blocking it. If the Commission is refraining from action, it is because it has lost its independence and is in the hands of the large Member States.

DCB: The Commission is the offspring of the European Council: it appoints its President and Commissioners, even though the European Parliament gives its consent. Historically, there was a strong Commission, as presided over by Jacques Delors (1985-1994) because François Mitterrand and Helmut Kohl delegated him to achieve the single Market and then the single currency. Delors therefore had the confidence and support of the Franco-German pairing. But after the Maastricht Treaty of 1991, the large States, including Great Britain, immunised by the Delors years, preferred to have weak Commissions. The European executive gradually became the secretariat of the Council. José Manuel Durao Barroso, the current President of the Commission, was appointed on a proposal from London as he was the incarnation of this new role given to the Commission, that of being a mediator between States. And since the creation of the post of President of the European Council in 2010, even that role is under dispute!

GV: The Commission now only puts forward a project if it has firstly obtained the approval of some large States, essentially France and Germany. Logically, this leads to the disappearance of the right of initiative. Now it is the States which hold this right in practice. Every time I ask the Commission about an abstention, it replies that it was not able to obtain the approval of one of the large States and that therefore there would be no point in entering into a battle that it considers to be lost in advance. This is totally false: to put forward a project creates a dynamic, especially in areas where the decision is by qualified majority.

DCB: The Commission could also rely on the European Parliament. If we were to amend its proposal with its agreement before it is even lodged with the Council of Ministers, that would create time for debate between, on one side, the governments and on the other side, the Commission and the Parliament. And furthermore, if we were able to rally the national parliaments to this common position, the debate would be "Europeanised".

GV: It's worse: the Commission is trying to convince the parliamentarians to change their mind rather than the Member States.

DCB: The Commissioners still see themselves too much as representing their country, which is tragic for the European executive. From the moment you are appointed Commissioner, you represent Europe and not your country in the Commission. It is true that we have the same problem in the Parliament. There are national delegations who behave like representatives of their State, especially if they are part of a government majority.

JQ: *That is the situation with the German delegation. On certain matters of national interest, the Greens have not hesitated to vote with the Liberals and the Christian Democrats. That was the case, in particular, in 2001, on the proposed directive liberalising takeover bids. On the French or Italian side, however, you would never see such behaviour. Ideology will always prevail over national concerns.*

113

DCB: That is not always true. During the German Presidency of the Union, in 1999, Gerhard Schröder, who was Chancellor at the time, asked Joschka Fischer, Foreign Minister and former leader of the Greens, to call me to ask me to support the German position during the vote on a proposal for a directive. Joschka told him that it would be a waste of effort. But it is true that governments put pressure on their MEPs, it is true of Germany, and also of Spain, as Zapatero, for example, forced the Spanish socialist delegation to vote in favour of the directive on the return of illegal immigrants when it did not wish to do so. Both European Parliament Members who did not follow the voting instruction were then not on the list of the PSOE (Partido Socialista Obrero Español – Spanish Socialist Workers Party) in 2009. It is a real problem because, if it behaves as a defender of national interests, the European Parliament will lose its credibility and legitimacy.

JQ: *The European Parliament is structurally "national", as the representatives are elected on a "national" basis. These movements are therefore not surprising. However, the Commission has for a long time been structurally European, despite its method of appointment (by governments). Is it not related to the personalities who make up the Commission who were largely chosen because they were politically weak?*

DCB: Exactly. I think the only way of giving power and independence to the President of the Commission would be to have him elected by universal suffrage, as proposed by the German Finance Minister, the Christian Democrat Wolfgang Schäuble. He would then become the true President of the Union and would have the necessary legitimacy to speak to governments on an equal footing.

GV: The European Parliament could also appoint him as a head of government in a parliamentary democracy.

DCB: Indeed, but there would at least have to be transnational lists so that the European Parliament is no longer simply the juxtaposition of different national electoral bodies. The person at the top of the transnational list who wins the elections would then automatically become the President of the Commission. But this could only be for a transitional period. Election by universal suffrage would be an unbelievable shock.

JQ: *How can a person who doesn't speak the language of his country be elected by universal suffrage?*

DCB: No one speaks the 23 languages of the Union. It would be enough to find anyone who speaks four or five languages. But I acknowledge that this could cause a problem in some countries. In my view, you have to look beyond this: after all, when I talk to the Greeks I do not speak their language and yet I am understood.

JQ: *Nevertheless, it means believing that the current division of national public areas could be transcended by an electoral mechanism.*

GV: That's true, but there are other reforms that can be introduced to bring about that common public area which is cruelly lacking. For example, in the manifesto, we propose that specific taxes would be paid into the European budget, creating a link between the citizens and the European political level, as the basis of any democratic system is the parliamentary control of taxes and expenditure.

DCB: The nation State means social security which protects you when you are ill, unemployed or retired, education which trains you and prepares you for the future, the army which defends you when you are attacked. There must therefore be a process of European integration which comes to pass through these policies.

JQ: *For example, why not mutualise part of unemployment insurance? That would enable transfers to be made between countries experiencing growth and the others, but would also involve the countries making the transfers in the development of the beneficiary States.*

GV: All sorts of systems can be imagined. But whatever system is chosen, we must be aware that, in order to be legitimate in the eyes of the people, a federal Europe must include an important social dimension.

It is clearly not a question of standardising from the bottom; it is not a question of asking the Dutch, for example, who have the best retirement system in the Union with a guaranteed pension representing approximately 60% of final salary, to abandon anything. We must simply define a valid minimum base of rights for all European countries even though differences remain.

In order to be viable, a federal State does not imply uniformity. That is the case for the United States, for example, where the wealth differential between the federated States is as large as within the euro zone. But for the time being, while the Union has harmonised its standards more than the United States, they have been much further on than we are in harmonising their policies, particularly due to a federal budget which is 23% of GDP. Our challenge is now to do the same thing in order to fight against this idea that Europe is limited to a single market, as Great Britain would like.

JQ: *As a matter of urgency, aren't the States in the euro zone in the process of creating an a-democratic monster? Thus a series of solutions ("six pack" then "two pack") gave powers to the European Commission over national budgets, which amounts to limiting the powers of the Parliaments, without any democratic counterweight being set in place. The same applies for the EFSF and the ESM which are more involved with the financial responsibility of States. The debate over the "Eurobonds" itself has got off to a bad start.*

There is still no question of allowing the Union to borrow on the markets under the control of the European Parliament, but of finding a mechanism which will allow States to run into debt cheaply due to the European signature. In short, without the federal leap, do we not risk entering a real technocratic dictatorship?

GV: In a crisis, we often patch things up, which ends up with questionable results. But this is a transitional stage and it is possible to come out of these makeshift solutions in an upwards direction, by creating a federal union which alone would allow democratic control. The order of things should not be reversed: first of all there was the British State, then British democracy. First of all there was the French State, then French democracy. It is not democracy which leads the State, it is the opposite and the movement is still carried by a bourgeois elite. The British example is very clear: until the middle of the 19th Century only 5 or 6% of men had the right to vote. It was not until 1918 that the vote became "universal", and 1928 until it was extended to women. I think therefore that it is false to say that it is necessary to create a functional democracy first for a European federation to emerge from it.

DCB: We must be careful of these historical parallels. We are no longer in the England or France of the 19th Century, we are living in open democratic societies. The decisions of the political elite should accompany a movement of society, which will

118

accelerate political dynamism. We cannot postpone the question of democracy until later, as that risks alienating the citizens of the Union further. But I acknowledge that democratisation is not a guarantee in itself that the people will identify with Europe, which is a fundamental factor if we want them to take it on. It is a complicated route, especially as we know that national identity was forged in many countries by revolution or a freedom fight, which is not the case of the European process, the civil wars which ravaged our continent were not the same...

GV: At the basis of revolutions is the will to be involved politically and economically in affairs and not to allow all the fruits of the country to fall into the hands of those in charge. That was what happened in the "Glorious Revolution" in England in 1688 or the French Revolution in 1789. Europe is not so far from such a model. It must no longer be reserved for governments alone, it must open up to its people.

DCB: Therefore you could look at what we propose in our manifesto as a revolution. But we must reinforce its basis which is the people. I think the main problem is that we are in a highly political debate, but it has not yet managed to mobilise the people.

GV: That is certainly because there is no European social or educational policy, areas where the people are directly involved.

DCB: That is why we are proposing, for example, the creation of a European social service so that everyone can work for one or two years in another European country. It would be financed by the European budget and companies and would enable everyone to become aware of the European reality. But we also have to deal with disenchantment when it comes to politics. The electoral results and participation show that there is a political crisis in Europe. Only elections considered to be crucial, such as the presidential elections in France or legislative elections in Germany, still bring the voters out.

GV: It's the same in the United States…

DCB: Some people say that the people don't want anything to do with the European elections because Europe is too far removed from their concerns. However, in the last municipal elections in Frankfurt, which were to elect the Mayor directly, participation was 36%! So Europe is too far away and the city is too near? We must be serious about this: disenchantment with politics does not only affect Europe. That brings us to the fundamental question of the European public area which can only be created by the drama of elections.

JQ: *The election of members to the European Parliament is not really a people's success story...*

DCB: That is because it takes place within a national framework, which does not create any dynamic in

European terms as you are not voting for a political majority at European level. It is simply a case of sanctioning or supporting the majority in place. We must put right this defect in construction. Possibly some MEPs would be elected on transnational lists which would force them to campaign in several countries. It could also be decided that the European party (conservatives of the EPP, liberals, socialists, Greens etc.) which comes first would automatically take the Presidency of the Commission, a post which should be merged with that of the President of the European Council. Thus, the President of the Union would be chosen in the European elections, which would create a true political dynamism. There would be one single campaign throughout Europe and not 27 national debates. Of course, it is also possible to elect the President of the Union by direct universal suffrage.

GV: It is also possible that you could be a candidate in several constituencies in different countries if there are no transnational lists which the majority of European MEPs do not want.

DCB: The simplest system would be for those putting themselves forward for the Presidency of the Union to be at the top of the list in all European countries.

GV: Or in some European countries, according to their choice. Having said that, I think that while the institutional question is important, the crucial point for the emergence of a European democracy, is taxation. If there is no direct source from the people, at the level of the European budget, we will never be able to create a European democracy.

JQ: *"No representation without taxation", to reverse the American saying...*

GV: If people are paying for something, then they will be interested in it...

DCB: Who will decide on the tax? That is political representation. So Guy is right.

GV: If is for that reason that the States refuse any direct taxation which would go into the European budget and not because it would lead to an increase in deductions as they claim, even if that is untrue. They want Europe to remain an international organisation which they pay into directly and therefore which they control without the people having their say. The power must be given back to the people, who will decide directly the ways in which they want to give it to Europe.

TOWARDS FEDERALISM

JQ: *Certainly, but neither the States nor the political parties want to give up any more sovereignty. We saw it in 2003, during the convention to prepare the European Constitution. National MEPs, in the majority, refused to move further forward with integration.*

GV: That's true, but we must remain aware that in reality we are not asking for the opinion of the electors! As I have already said, they have a choice between the Eurosceptic lists, on the right or the left, and the conventional parties satisfied with a status quo which has no federal aspect, contrary to the claims of the anti-Europeans…

DCB: Even Europe Ecology, when it is a matter of deciding something on Europe, prefer to hide or vote against. We saw their attitude at the time of the vote in France on the European Stability Mechanism (ESM): EELV (Europe Ecology, the Greens) abstained!

GV: That is why we need a radical pro-European force proposing a federal union.

DCB: We can change the parameters, we can come out of the current euro-pessimism by offering the people a clear vision of the future, which we call the "postnational revolution", and which can help us out of the crisis.

123

JQ: *How can this leap actually be made? Calling a new convention which will draw up a new treaty?*

GV: A convention which is not supported by the people will have no chance of getting anywhere.

DCB: We propose that after the 2014 election the European Parliament should proclaim itself as the Constituent Assembly, in agreement with the Council of Ministers, the other legislative chamber, and should draw up a draft European Constitution which will not be a repeat of the current treaties, as was the case in 2004. This text must define the principles of a federal Europe and be brief. It must be approved by referendum in all the countries by a double majority (majority of States and citizens). The States which vote "no" must then decide, again by referendum, whether to remain in this new federal Europe or to leave it.

GV: It will be the "Philadelphia moment", when in 1785, the United States decided to move from the confederation to the federation. To get round the rule of unanimity, they decided that the new constitution would be adopted by a majority of 9/13ths. Why that figure? Because nine States were in favour of abandoning unanimity while four were against. The latter had the choice: either accept the 9/13ths rule, or leave. Rhode Island, after hesitating, was the last of the thirteen States to accept it.

DCB: The German Grundgesetz of 1949 was accepted by all the Länder except for Bavaria. But it is still part of the German Republic and complies with the Basic Law…If we do not do the same thing in Europe, we won't come through. I acknowledge that there will be a problem if Germany or France refuses the new Constitution, but we have to take that risk. It is essential that at a given moment, the people state clearly what they want and decide their future.

JQ: *Federalism won't happen with 27…*

GV: It will happen with the countries which decide to go with it…

DCB: In 1990, no one thought that the euro would happen with 17 countries. There is a magnetic force of the Union that cannot be denied. The States and the people know that they cannot protect themselves alone or have influence in the world of today. I am sure that the people will choose Europe.
Even the British?

DCB: They have to make a choice. Either stay in Europe or try to become the 51st State of the United States.

JQ: *They could also remain and try to block any progress.*

DCB: In the constituent process we propose, that will no longer be possible. I look forward to this double British referendum. It is not "I want my money back", it is "you get nothing back". It will be the same for Sweden, the Czech Republic or Slovenia who have to decide whether to remain alone or join the majority.

GV: That will be their choice!

DCB: I am absolutely confident. If we reach this constituent process, at that revolutionary moment, I will be surprised if the people of those countries decide to leave.

JQ: *And you believe that a federation with 27 members could function efficiently?*

DCB: In Philadelphia, there were 13 American States. If you had told them that one day there would be 50, they would never have believed it….

GV: …and they are more unified with 50 than with 13! We have to come out of this vision of a Europe of nation States where the force of numbers plays a role. Now we are talking about a federal Europe, with shared sovereignty, and public opinion which will be separate from that of the States. It will be the Europe of the people, a postnational Europe.

DCB: But that Europe won't come about until 2015 or 2016.

GV: Why not?

DCB: It will be far too early. Already, we have to challenge all the political families, whether they are pro-Europeans who dare not see it through, or anti-Europeans, to provoke a debate within all the public opinions in the Union. That is why we are publishing our manifesto in several countries at the same time. We are challenging the political parties to respond and explain their own plans. Of course, with no guarantee of success.

JQ: *It is obviously not certain that you will get a response. We are in a period of withdrawal, of shutting things out, not being open to others, no political courage...*

DCB: Well, that is why we are stirring things up. In 1789, the universal Declaration of the Rights of Man, was very idealistic!

GV: What is idealistic and unrealistic is to expect that the status quo can continue.

JQ: *The problem is that today, there is no longer a pro-European force, like the MRP in France in the 1950s, the German CDU until 2000 etc. Don't you risk falling into a vacuum?*

DCB: That is a risk. That is why Guy Verhofstadt imagines a broad pro-European alliance for the next European elections which will bring together the liberals, the Greens, the socialists and the conservatives.

JQ: *So it's a case of coming out of the right-left axis and creating a "pro" and anti" European axis?*

DCB: Not "pro" and "anti". His idea is to launch a "European Federalist" party, against the Europeans who are for the status quo and the Eurosceptics.

The problem is that this idea only functions with me…That is not the political reality. However, one could imagine a "European pact", setting out the organisation of a transpartisan primary election to appoint the person who will be the candidate of the federalists for the Presidency of the Commission. The lists will be presented independently of each other, but if together those who signed this pact have the majority in the European Parliament, they will impose their candidate upon the European Council. This process will enable some millions of European citizens to be mobilised, before the European election , who can choose between the liberal Guy Verhofstadt, the ecologist Dany Cohn-Bendit, the socialist Martin Schulz, the liberal Sylvie Goulard, the Swedish conservative Carl Bildt etc. Here is another idealism, I have not given up hope of one day seeing the European Green party becoming a true European ecologist and federalist party.

JQ: *In that case, the right/left splits are not denied.*

DCB: They do exist, you must not deny them. Third option: the Greens, the liberals, and those who wish to, quickly propose a resolution to the European Parliament asking the Commission to reform the polling method so that a European citizen can be a candidate in several countries, which offers the possibility of having European list leaders.

JQ: *In order to create a transnational political dynamism, why not give the right to vote to European citizens in all national elections? That would force the candidates to take account of the European dimension in their national campaigns.*

DCB: In the manifesto, we propose that European citizenship would allow that. A true European passport could even be created, without referring to the State on its cover…

GV: Who are the French? They are Europeans who live in the French area. We propose a reinterpretation of nationality.

DCB: People are still surprised that I was elected once in France, and once in Germany. Everyone thinks I have dual nationality, but that is not the case: I am German. But in the European elections I can be a candidate everywhere. This must also be the case for national ballots.

JQ: *While the French left now seems less reticent towards the prospect of political Union, it sees that financial solidarity is a prerequisite, whereas for the Germans, it is the opposite…*

DCB: There is a contradiction in the position of the French left. Schengen illustrates it. Unlike the right, it does not wish to question this area of free movement, but wants States alone to judge the need to suspend it in the event of an "influx" of foreigners. The European Parliament thinks the exact opposite: the evaluation of a situation of "tension" at a border must be European to avoid giving rise to national populism. Above all, this will allow democratic control by the Parliament, as a national decision means a sovereign decision of governments alone. Finally, the French refusal shows a real mistrust with regard to the Community institutions; it is as if they think that the Union, by its nature, wanted to harm States, which is completely stupid… Today the French border or the German border is the European border. The protection of borders, the policies of asylum and immigration, can be debated but within the European area. To believe that we will be protected by national borders makes no sense. French defence of sovereignty, whether it is on the right or the left, is certainly still well and truly present.

GV: However, it is important to remember that there is another French tradition, that of Jean Monnet, Robert Schuman and Jacques Delors who wanted the advent of European federalism. To answer your question, I believe political union should not be set against financial solidarity. You have to do both at the same time. I would even go further and say that solidarity is a basic part of political union. The Germans and the French have to come out of their trenches. If they do not, it will be disastrous!

DCB: In Germany, there is a huge gap between words and actions. While the Germans say they want political union, in their actions they often behave exactly like the French, as we have seen on Schengen, whereas on the other hand, they do all they can to give maximum powers to the European Commission on the control of national budgets. That is a contradiction. In the same way, on foreign policy, you cannot say that consistency reigns. You cannot ask for political union and at the same time abstain from the UN Security Council, alone against all Europeans, on the intervention in Libya. Berlin has shown that it is incapable of understanding the political dimension of the European decision. Political union, for the Merkel government merely hides a total lack of strategic thought! On the French side, it is no clearer. Financial solidarity is necessary in a political union, but that implies a challenge to sovereignty including on social matters, which Paris does not want to hear about.

JQ: *Even if we consider that the Germans are not totally straight as a die, is there not a fundamental difference in approach between the Germans and the*

French with regard to federalism? For the French, federalism is basically removing power from Paris to the benefit of the Union, whereas for the Germans, federalism is the certainty of being protected by a higher level without their actual sovereignty being affected.

GV: This is to do with the fact that the French State is unitary and centralised whereas the German State is federal. A federal State sees in European federalism a guarantee that everyone does what he must at his level. It is not a case of creating a super-State centralised in Brussels which will do everything. It will certainly mean a convergence of policies, but each will retain room for manoeuvre.

DCB: The first expression of the sovereignty of this European federalism will be a true European budget capable of supporting national policies while respecting the autonomy of national budgets. In the United States, they have a federal budget which is 23% of the American GDP, with total autonomy of State budgets. Even better: there is a "no bail out" clause which prohibits States from being rescued for default of payment.

JQ: *It was in 1841 that the United States decided to stop rescuing federated States which were in default of payment.*

DCB: Indeed, up to that date, the federal State came to the rescue of the federated States. It stopped at that time. California had to come out of that situation on its own, but we must not forget that several social budgets are paid into by the federal budget which also invests in the States. The same thing should happen in Europe. Put the counters back to zero, create a credible federal budget, let's say 10% of the Community GDP, or 1200 billion euros per annum, and give ourselves credible federal policies.

GV: It is the only way of coming out of the euro zone crisis. What is the difference between the United States, Japan and us? They have a budget and a credible central authority.

DCB: With a serious democratic control.

JQ: *Jens Weidmann, the President of the Bundesbank, has explained that there were two possible models. The Maastricht model, which is close to the American model, where each State operates alone to manage its accounts correctly. As no one can help, there must be a "golden rule" to avoid overspending. The other model is that of the German federal State: common financial responsibility which implies strong political union. But Weidmann does not take his reasoning to its conclusion, as he omits that in both models there is a substantial budget.*

GV: Indeed, the Maastricht model can only function if there is a budget.

DCB: This budget has to be financed by own resources, that is European taxes.

GV: For the people, nothing will change: they will still pay their 40% or 45% of fiscal and parafiscal charges, only one part will go to Europe and the other to the States. That is what happens in the United States.

JQ: *The States are certainly not following that line as they even want to reduce the amount of the Community budget for the period from 2014 to 2020*

GV: With an amount of 1% of the GDP (Gross Domestic Product) of the Community, what is the credibility of the Community budget? You are answering the question by asking it. To get round the problem of the necessary solidarity and mutualisation of resources, the governments have taken another route which consists of imposing a strong budgetary rigidity upon States, as that is where the reality of the power lies. This identical discipline for everyone has no sense. In the United States, the federated States are not subject to the same rules. If the market has confidence in the United States and lends at low rates, it is because it has the guarantee of the federal budget behind it.

JQ: *The American debt we are talking about is that of the Federal State and not of the federated States or local authorities..*

GV: That is the point I am making. If the Union had a federal budget of a size equivalent to that of the United States, we would not have experienced the debt crisis we are currently dealing with. The American debt, taking all levels together, is much greater than the euro zone debt, but the United States has no problem with financing, any more than Japan, whose debt exceeds 200% of GDP! In a federal Europe with a budget, the fact that Greece or Spain has problems would not affect the whole Union, as those countries would have the same importance as California or Rhode Island in relation to the United States. It is because we do not have a federal State with a serious federal budget, with its own resources, with a debt guaranteed by that federal State that a small economy such as that of Greece representing 2% of the GDP of the euro zone can set off a global crisis. The solution is clear, it is patently obvious.

JQ: *The founding fathers of the European Union had planned from the 1950s that the budget of the Union financed by own resources would gain ground. These resources consisted of customs duties paid on entering the Union, "levies" on imported agricultural products and a percentage of VAT. But these resources, which still exist, have decreased and been marginalised by a contribution calculated on the GDP of each State which allows them to block any increase at each negotiation of the "financial perspectives" every seven or five years. We have to move on from this system by empowering European resources.*

DCB: More and more is being asked of Europe and at the same time it is being given less and less. Governments see the European budget as a hated imposition. It is a festival of national egotism. One good example is the Netherlands which, in 2006, obtained an increase from 10 to 25% in the administrative tax they charge for imports to the European internal market, but which enter through the port of Rotterdam! In fact, they are collecting a tax on a European tax. At the time, Guy Verhofstadt, who was Prime Minister of Belgium, said nothing, as the port of Antwerp, the other main port of entry into the Union, benefited from the same treatment.

GV: That's true.

DCB: We should also understand that the sums not spent by the Union during the year do not increase the budget for the following year, but are returned to the States. In their draft budget, they make an estimate and include it in their resources! This does not encourage spending.

JQ: *The Community budget has therefore become full of holes...*

DCB: If this budget were financed by resources which no longer depended on the States, they would benefit, as they would save the sums which they pay every year (20 billion for France, 21 billion for Germany etc.). To finance the Community budget, the VAT resource could be increased (a small part going to the Union budget) and carbon taxes or taxes on financial transactions could be created. The mobile telephone or internet sectors could also be taxed in a specific way. This would give real political power to the Community institutions (Commission, European Parliament, Council of Ministers) and legitimise them in the eyes of public opinion.

GV: Some expenditure could also be mutualised such as research or defence. Today, the accumulated military budgets represent half of American expenditure, which is already huge. But on the ground, we are only capable of carrying out 10% of American operations because our resources are dispersed; in each country there is an information service, a strategic and tactical capacity, a medical service, in short we do the same thing 27 times!

JQ: *Is the keystone of monetary union therefore not so much political union as a sizeable budget?*

DCB: No, on the contrary. A sizeable budget implies a government which decides how to use it. That is the whole problem with people who talk about political union without providing for a budget.

JQ: *How can France be convinced that federalism will not weaken it?*

DCB: France thinks that it has power but it no longer has that power. You just need to see the reactions to the proposal of Michel Rocard, the former prime minister, to get rid of the nuclear deterent in order to make savings. He is right: The threat today comes from terrorism, local guerrillas against whom nuclear weapons are of no help. Nuclear weapons are also no use for military interventions of a "humanitarian" nature as was the case in the Balkans, Libya, and perhaps in Syria. Nuclear weapons are just an illusion of power whereas we know they will not be used for anything. There is also the permanent seat of France in the UN Security Council which it holds on to, but it has never once used its right of veto. So during the second Iraq war, France gained against the United States diplomatically by obtaining a majority in the Security Council with the support of Germany.

GV: In the Manifesto we therefore propose that the seats in the international authorities become European seats.

JQ: *In Europe, with regard to foreign policy, is it not, at best, the risk of paralysis, with the lowest bidder always prevailing, and at worst, alignment with the United States? In 2003, the majority of European countries were for the war in Iraq.*

GV: Quite simply because Europe does not exist… what is NATO? It is an organisation of nation states dominated by the United States which holds two thirds of its military capacity.

DCB: However NATO was not sent to Iraq, as the majority was not in agreement. That is why we had a "coalition of the willing" and not NATO. That being so, you are right to emphasise the deep concerns of France faced with a European foreign policy. But I am convinced that it will be different when we have a true Europe which will define a policy of common interest, which will not be just the national policies added together. Today we can allow ourselves different views over Libya, as we did not have to take a decision together.

GV: Without diplomacy and European defence, we cannot reach a common decision. During the European Council in Spain in 2002, chaired by José Maria Aznar and which I attended as Prime Minister, we spoke about Iraq for two minutes. Jacques Chirac and Tony Blair intervened to say that it was not necessary given the divergence in points of view. It was the same for Libya. Only a European defence force will make us define common positions.

JQ: *You cannot deny that, apart from France and Great Britain, Europeans think of themselves first of all as a large Switzerland or a small China and not as the new United States of America. Europe is a continent of old countries which has abdicated any idea of power...*

DCB: Neither France nor Great Britain now has the resources to fulfil their ambitions. In Libya, the Americans had to provide the ammunition. The old powers refuse to face up to the reality of the world of today. Our powerlessness in the face of reality in the war in Libya was only a repeat of the experience during the war in the Balkans. A war only an hour's flight from the European capitals! A war where the European army was incapable of stopping the massacres in Sarajevo, Vukovar, Dubrovnik and Srebrenica. The lesson is clear, only a European army, which is mobile, and technologically advanced, will be able in future to defend both our values and our sovereignty. In addition, a European army would be cheaper. Instead of the two million or so soldiers we currently have, we would have an army of around 350 000 or 400 000 soldiers capable of intervening in the world of today if required. Furthermore, we could set up a European civil task force – as proposed by the Commissioner Michel Barnier – so that it is able to intervene in the event of ecological or industrial disasters.

NATIONAL IDENTITY AND EUROPE

JQ: *Is a federal Europe possible while there is no European identity, but a juxtaposition of national identities?*

GV: What nationalists do is to reduce identity to language, ethnic group or race. In actual fact, people have multiple identities – family, local, national, historical, sexual, political etc. It is that group of identities, in layers, that makes the individual unique. National identity does not predominate and erase all the others. So in the modern world, individuals can choose their own identity. To talk about a "European identity" is falling into the nationalists' trap.

JQ: *Can we at least imagine European patriotism?*

DCB: I would dare to talk about European patriotism. Habermas developed the idea of "constitutional patriotism" which means not identifying with a national or geographical identity, but with its values, avoiding the trap of nationalism. This works perfectly for Europe: you can be a patriot of Europe as a political realisation.

JQ: *Would the political structure therefore partly determine our identity?*

DCB: No, it determines our relationship with the political area. The European citizen wants to be protected against war, disease, the economic crisis, global warming, the ecological crisis, and the disintegration of living spaces by unregulated globalisation. From that point, the political area which best fulfils that function is clearly Europe.

JQ: *Is it not really a case of creating a "nation of nations" to use Jean Monnet's expression?*

DCB: To a certain extent. That would be civilizational progress.

GV: Human history shows that we have moved on, clearly without linearity, from tribal societies, to regions, kingdoms, and nation States. Now we are organised at continental level, which is a move forward in European civilisation.

DCB: The nation State was progress compared with feudalism, the supranational area is progress compared with the nation States. Now we must create a subcontinental political area.

JQ: *However, regional assertions have never been so strong, particularly in Europe...*

GV: It is not against the idea of a multicultural Europe. European federalism rightly takes account of these regional sentiments. Germany shows that you can have a strong federal State with strong Länder.

JQ: *That is certainly true, but the Länder are not constituted on an ethnic and linguistic basis. In some countries, like Belgium, Spain or Italy, the assertion of independence is based on the idea that only areas that are ethnically, linguistically or economically homogeneous can function effectively.*

GV: Federalism means ethnic groups, religions, and different languages can live together in the same political area with solidarity.

JQ: *Regionalism today does not show solidarity: regional assertions are often based on the idea that one is bled dry economically by poorer people who do not belong to your community. Look at Flanders, for example...*

GV: This phenomenon, which I do not dispute, can be explained by the fact that the regions have had to fight for their autonomy in a centralised State which denied their identity. In Germany, in the United States, the process was the opposite: it was the States which decided to come together and there was not the same phenomenon of egotism.

DCB: However, we should state that German federalism in its democratic expression, that which recognises regional sovereignties, was built after 1945. Before that, Germany was founded on the dominance of Prussia. The fact remains that one cannot deny the emergence of regional egotism. As the nation State of today is not capable of providing protection from globalisation, some people think that a smaller area would be more efficient, including against those who are not from the same region and who are also seen as a threat. This is clearly false: the regional area offers no additional protection, it is even the exact opposite. If a State is not able to resist globalisation, how could a microregion do so? The right area is the European area which alone can defend our way of life against the other large continental areas.

JQ: *What makes Europe what it is? What binds Europeans together?*

GV: If you take a walk in Europe, you can see everywhere the architecture is the same, the towns are similar.

DCB: You can find the Italian piazza in Poland.

GV: The colours of Italy in Sweden.

JQ: *And Christianity?*

GV: Not at all! The Bosnians and Albanians are Europeans and they are not Christians. They became Muslims because that meant they paid lower taxes to the Ottomans. Which also shows the cultural importance of taxation …

DCB: The Christian religion plays a role in European history, that is obvious. But parallel to that, the fight against the hold of religion, the separation of Church and State or at least the private and public spheres and the emergence of democracy are also part of European civilisation. There is also the Jewish diaspora which is an integral part of European culture.

GV: Elias Canetti, who won the Nobel Prize for Literature, begins his autobiography "Die gerettete Zunge" by explaining that he was born in Ruse, Rucuk in Turkish, on the Danube on the Bulgarian-Romanian border, a town where seven languages were spoken: Bulgarian, Romanian, Russian, because in all good families there were Russian women who came to work, Ladino, a Spanish dialect, because there was the Sephardic Jewish diaspora which had settled in Ruse, Catalan because there were also Catalan Jews, Turkish, because it was the Ottoman Empire and there were Turkish minorities, and German, because at the weekend they went to Vienna. That was the Europe that was destroyed during the two world wars.

DCB: Since 1945, Islam has moved in and become stronger in Europe. Today there are more Muslims in Europe than there are Dutch people. However, one should say that Europe is evolving and Islam will have the same fate as Christianity which had to accept, not without violent conflicts, separation between the private and public sectors. Jews are even returning to Europe. Today more than 50 000 Israelis live in Berlin. All of that is Europe.

145

JQ: *Jacques Le Goff wrote in "Was Europe born in the Middle Ages?" that Turkey does not belong to this European civilizational area which is Christian. For him, Europe stops at the Bosphorus.*

GV: That is contrary to the whole history of Europe! The Ottomans, who occupied the Balkans for 450 years, have played a fundamental role in our culture. The Ottoman Empire was one of the basic factors of European politics.

JQ: *The enemy is still an important element of foreign policy...*

GV: They were not an enemy! There were many more links and alliances between the British and the Sublime Porte than between France and England. The Europeans even helped the Ottomans in their fight against Russia when Russia wanted to extend its hold over the Black Sea...

DCB: We must also remember that the Muslims were in Spain for 750 years and that the European colonial empires included a large part of the Muslim world in the 19th and 20th Centuries. Today, the Muslim world is looking for its place in Europe, a place it will have fewer problems finding thanks to secularity. European civilisation now includes a part of the Muslim world, that is the reality. And that represents an opportunity: while we are fighting against radical and totalitarian Islam, we are not at war with the Muslim religion.

JQ: *Is it for that reason that you are both in favour of Turkey joining the Union?*

DCB: We have missed the boat. We gave the Turks a flat refusal which turned them away from Europe. Current developments are very worrying, as the Islamist government is openly violating the fundamental values of Europe more and more, which is moving them away from any prospect of accession.

JQ: *Today in Europe, many political parties are playing more on aggravating cultural differences, as was shown in the French debate on national identity initiated by Nicolas Sarkozy, former French Head of State.*

DCB: Unfortunately, the political parties have a tendency to stick to public opinion.

GV: They ask themselves what does the public think and they decide to think the same, which of course, reinforces prejudices. However, I think politicians should have an idea, a vision, a project and try to convince the public that it is right. Public opinion is created. Today democracy is reduced to populism too frequently.

DCB: The question is whether or not you gamble on the intelligence of societies. A new type of dialogue must be created between the politicians who have a vision and the citizens who debate it. That is what will allow a public European area to be created. For the moment, the only questions that are asked are to find out what Angela Merkel or François Hollande think…

JQ: *Europeans hardly have any feeling of belonging to Europe. Some think the only way of creating that feeling is to fight for Europe, undergo the test of blood? What do you think?*

GV: Did the First and Second World War not do that?

DCB: It is the test of blood and fire which led some mad visionaries to propose the creation of the Union, as we could not continue to kill one another if we belonged to the same civilisation. As Stéphane Hessel rightly said, "Europe was born at Buchenwald". Europe was born in the trenches of Verdun and in the death camps. Europe has already experienced the test of fire. The specific aspect of Europe, which is at odds with History, is to create a geopolitical area without war and without one country dominating.

GV: We are banking more on intelligence and reason…

DCB: It is the strength and weakness of the European project.

JQ: *So it is not necessary to send our soldiers to die in Iran or elsewhere for us to have the feeling of being Europeans?*

DCB: I am not saying there will never be military intervention in particular situations, but Europe is not a warmongering project which needs bloodshed in order to exist. We are an area where conflicts are settled by law, an economic and social area which aims to increase the well-being of everyone, an area which exports standards and not violence. In concrete terms, to reinforce this feeling of belonging, we propose, for example, that everyone is able to go and work for at least one year in another European country with a minimum guaranteed salary.

GV: In the 18th Century, young German intellectuals had to make a trip to Italy, it was essential. Also, there were no borders and they did not need a passport.

DCB: It is not by war but by common experience that we will create this feeling of belonging.

GV: Your question presumes that one day a foreign force will want to seize power in Europe which will force Europeans to react together to defend themselves. But that will never happen! Fortunately there is no longer a Soviet Union which threatens world equilibrium in this way.

JQ: *In short, if we understand you correctly, there is nothing between postnational Europe and the nation*

State; the worst scenario: return to the nation State, which according to you, will ensure disappearance from the world map...

DCB: Let's be clear. Europe is our lifebelt in the storm of crises we are now facing. I think we have shown the complexity of the financial, ecological and identity crises. And it seems that the utopia of a federal Europe would be much more than simply a "spare wheel". Federal Europe is what I call a "plausible utopia". That is perhaps the last political utopia which could emerge from our continent which has been savagely devastated by totalitarian and murderous utopias. The emancipation of the Europeans "will be the work of the people themselves."

GV: If Daniel and I, despite our political paths which are so different – starting with radical neo-liberalism for me and libertarian radicalism for him – have felt the need to write this manifesto, it is because by understanding how serious the stakes are, we have made our way towards this plausible utopia, that of a postnational federal Europe. It is in no way an illusion. It is a real political project by which we can find again ways of matching our ambitions and dealing with the future.

CPSIA information can be obtained at www.ICGtesting.com
Printed in the USA
LVOW051547181212

312260LV00001B/51/P

9 781479 261888